# ANTHROPOLOGY
## A PERSPECTIVE
## ON MAN

# ANTHROPOLOGY A PERSPECTIVE ON MAN

Robert T. Anderson

**Mills College**

**Wadsworth Publishing Company, Inc.**
**Belmont, California**

ISBN–0–534–00148–3
L. C. Cat. Card No. 79–182067
Printed in the United States of America

1 2 3 4 5 6 7 8 9 10–76 75 74 73 72

For Stan, Mary, and Stefan

# Preface

This book is one man's answer to those who ask "What is anthropology?" It is meant to be easy to understand, yet sophisticated. It is also meant to have relevance to real people and their problems in our time. I have, in fact, put into writing a course on anthropology as I teach it to undergraduates. Student reactions and suggestions have done much to give it shape. The result is, I hope, a book that students will find useful and enjoy.

I owe much to my teachers as well as to my students. Among them, Theodore D. McCown in particular did much to shape me as an anthropologist. He inspired by his own example a dedication to disciplined thought, an openness to new ideas, and a commitment to humane values. His untimely death is cause for deep sorrow.

Students and teachers alike depend on much that they normally take for granted: the dedicated personnel and expensive resources of a modern institution of higher learning. Mills College is such a place, and I acknowledge with gratitude the great debt I owe for unfailing support and encouragement.

Through the courtesy of Jack G. Arnold of Wadsworth Publishing Company, the manuscript for this book was read by Edward Norbeck of Rice University, Bernard J. Siegel of Stanford University, Peter Chroman of the College of San Mateo, and George V. Shkurkin of the University of California, Berkeley. I profited greatly from their perceptive comments and helpful criticisms and extend to each my most sincere thanks.

Robert T. Anderson

# Contents

## Levels of Human Evolution

(The space allotted on this chart to the various epochs is not proportional to their actual duration.)

| Epochs of the Cenozoic Era | Related Living Forms of Prehistoric Grades | Grades of Primate Evolution | Stages of Cultural Evolution | Related Surviving Forms of Prehistoric and Historic Stages |
|---|---|---|---|---|
|  |  |  | industrial civilization | e.g., Soviet Union, United States |
|  |  |  | archaic civilization | e.g., Nepal, Tibet, Kanuri of Bornu (Africa) |
|  |  |  | Neolithic | horticultural villages, e.g., Hopi, Papuans (New Guinea) |
| Recent | man | *sapiens* | Mesolithic | hunting and gathering bands, e.g., Bushmen, Eskimo |
|  |  |  | Upper Paleolithic | *all extinct* |
| Upper Pleistocene | *all extinct* | *neanderthalensis* | Middle Paleolithic | *all extinct* |
| Middle Pleistocene | *all extinct* | *erectus* | Lower Paleolithic | *all extinct* |
| Lower Pleistocene | *all extinct* | *australopithecine* | Proto-Paleolithic | *all extinct* |
| Pliocene | *all extinct* | *ramapithecine* | *no available information* | *all extinct* |
| Miocene | chimpanzee, gorilla | *dryopithecine* | proto-culture | e.g., chimpanzee behavior |
| Oligocene | macaque, gibbon | *pithecine* |  | e.g., macaque behavior |
| Eocene | lemur, tarsier | *prosimian* |  | e.g., lemur behavior |
| Paleocene | tree shrew | primitive prosimian | *no culture* | e.g., tree shrew behavior |

# 1 The Science of Man

Anthropology is more than a science. It is a way of life. Of course, any scholarly discipline becomes a way of life for its practitioners, and one expects scholars to emerge from their studies with distinctive self-images and world views which integrate their professional concerns and activities with their lives as wholes.

A way of life is something to be shared. Man loses his humanity if he somehow removes himself or is removed from the give and take of family, friends, and community. After eighteen years in a solitary cell, the consciousness of Charles Dickens' Dr. Manette had shriveled to his fingertips and the dull attention he gave to shoes he made in the dark. Only deep in his innermost being could he still find a faint afterglow of the person he once had been. Restored to society, he became once again a human being, psychologically scarred, but a person, not a thing.

To live as a person is to share. For a scientist, this includes sharing the special findings and understandings of his discipline. It means sharing with other scientists. Dr. Frankenstein is purely a creature of fiction. A real scientist drys up if he isolates himself in his laboratory, for his own achievement is dependent upon the wide-ranging exchange of findings and ideas. It means sharing with students as well, for only in that way can the discipline continue to thrive and grow. It means sharing with the whole of society, because science is concerned with a reality that concerns us all.

The sharing one does as a scientist may take many forms, ranging from an informal give and take between colleagues at their work to the writing of formal articles and books. No form of sharing, however, is more important than teaching. In the classroom and lecture hall more than in any other scholarly arena, a discipline faces its destiny. Failure in teaching, failure to attract young talent and new-born interest, can render a subject moribund in a generation. Success brings fresh new minds to the task, and stimulates the stimulators as teachers themselves are rejuvenated.

Teaching is hardest at the introductory level. There is so much a student ought to be told and encouraged to explore that it is difficult to know where to begin and how to proceed. The great majority of anthropology textbooks are organized around a recitation of what has been achieved through each of the various research strategies in use or around a list of the findings in each major subfield of the discipline. Thus, the student is told, topic by topic, something of each of the major research strategies and subject categories of the discipline.

A topical approach to anthropology more or less breaks the subject down into two major subdivisions, *physical anthropology* and *cultural anthropology*. Because the training needed for each is very demanding and rather specialized, most anthropologists work almost entirely in either the one or the other, not in both. That is, as concerns original research, one person cannot normally hope to make contributions in both areas. Keeping abreast of developments in anthropology as a whole is quite another matter, however, and while Europeans in general let the two subfields drift far apart, with physical anthropology under the faculty of medicine or biology and cultural under the social sciences, in America they have always been united.

Physical anthropologists are biologists or paleontologists specializing in the study of subhuman Primates, fossil man, racial biology, and human genetics. They investigate monkey and ape behavior for clues to human society. They work on the anatomy of prehistoric fossils to find clues to the evolution of the human body and its ongoing modification. From racial morphology and population genetics, they investigate the significance of race in biological terms, a different view from that of race as a social or cultural problem. And always, they concern themselves with the effect of culture on body function as well as the converse.

Cultural anthropologists focus upon socially learned human behavior and its products. The subject is very large, however, so specialized subfields have grown up, each more or less discrete because the questions each asks and the methods each uses are distinctive. Some, for example, specialize in the study of language, probing into the way languages change over time, the way language differences can function as part of social and political interaction, the way language affects perception and cognition. As a field of study, this specialty requires technical training beyond what other anthropologists get, and the problems the discipline encompasses are correspondingly discrete to a greater or lesser extent. Because some who work in this area are not trained anthropologists, it is probably best to designate the field as *anthropological linguistics*.

For the same reason, *prehistoric archeology* distinguishes anthropologists who collect their data by digging from other archeologists, who work within the framework of classics, Near Eastern studies, or history, and therefore have access to information in written documents. Prehistoric archeologists turn up skeletal material as well as the artifacts of earlier societies, so some work as physical anthropologists on problems of *paleoan-*

*thropology,* the study of prehistoric anatomy. Mostly, however, they work as cultural anthropologists who cannot get into subjects that require living informants, but can learn much about the past from excavating houses, settlements, tools, and other durable materials.

Other subfields of cultural anthropology require training in sister disciplines. *Psychological anthropology* is especially concerned with the way in which individuals develop personalities consistent with the values and demands of their culture, but similarities and differences in psychological attributes, including perception and intelligence, are also studied. Training in psychology is clearly necessary. *Economic anthropology* is a specialization in primitive and peasant economic systems as well as the human factor in economic activities at any level. At first quite independent of economics as a discipline, in recent years formal training in economics has proved useful and even necessary. The relationship between *political anthropology* and political science or law has become similar as anthropological sophistication in the study of primitive government and of political theory has grown. Training in law or political science is increasingly requisite.

The overlap of all these subfields except archeology with the subfield of *ethnology* is perhaps an indication of the central place ethnology occupies within cultural anthropology. The study of social life in all its variety and complexity, it relies primarily upon the observations of field workers who live with the people they study, know their language, and systematically record what they see and experience. Ethnology thus incorporates not only linguistics, psychological anthropology, economic anthropology, and political anthropology but more as well. It includes concentrations on any of a wide range of topics, including religion, material culture, art, music, literature, role behavior, class structure, and the institutions of family, community, and other social groups. Ethnologists may study how a culture is integrated into a functioning whole, how items of culture have diffused from one society to another, how cultures change over time, or still other problems that kindle their interest.

It is important for anthropologists to know what is being done in each of these areas of the discipline. It is appropriate to spend time on every one of them. However, a serious objection may be raised when such topics and specialties are used as the table of contents—the order of presentation—of a textbook. Just as a hiker cannot see the forest when he gets too close to the trees, the student loses sight of the perspective of anthropology when he moves chapter by chapter from one topic to the next. Worse, he not only loses perspective, he loses interest. This is apparent to all, including the writers of textbooks. But those who would introduce neophytes to anthropology are caught on the horns of a dilemma. If they organize in terms of the larger perspective of anthropology, their students come away with gaps in their command of the parts.

To this dilemma there is no solution. Mastering a science is inherently difficult at the beginning, where the first parts must be learned in ignorance of the rest. As I sat down to write about anthropology, however, I decided against the normal textbook approach. In what follows, my aim is to give as much as possible to the beginner of that overall view of the world that the professional gains during many years of hard work. Rather than write about anthropology, I chose to write about man as he looks to the anthropologist. Rather than write about anthropological techniques used to learn about human behavior, I chose to write about behavior as such, discussing techniques when they were essential to explaining the viewpoint.

The result is a book about what man is. But while I do not have chapters on each of the various fields and topics as such, I could not write about man without bringing them into the discussion. They are there, but in bits and pieces brought together as needed for the narrative rather than as determined by encyclopedic requirements. What is lost in systematic and thorough coverage of anthropology as a discipline is gained, hopefully, in a systematic and thorough coverage of man in an anthropological perspective. In my view, this is putting first things first. It also makes for much more interesting reading.

I write, then, about man as he looks to an anthropologist. The result is necessarily a personal statement. It is my perspective at this particular time in my own personal growth. Others might write very differently. It is a mistake to assume that all anthropologists see their discipline and the object of their investigations in the same way, although by identifying ourselves as anthropologists, we all confess to some sharing. We see certain nineteenth century scholars as our academic grandfathers. Edward Burnett Tylor in England and Lewis Henry Morgan in the United States, in particular, staked claim for us to culture as our field of inquiry. But as a century and more has passed, different paths have been followed in different centers of scholarship, and within each center individuals have engaged in their own unique pursuits. So, while all anthropologists recognize a kinship of interest and expertise, each in the final analysis is different. Look, then, at anthropology and at man as I see him. Let it be your beginning. You too will make a journey which in the end will have been yours alone. I only hope to get you off to a good start.

My English teacher at Oakland's Fremont High School is only a vague memory now, a faceless body whose very name I have forgotten. It shames me to be so ungrateful. She worked with sympathetic devotion to get some of us into college, yet we didn't seem to realize how much she cared. Her assignment was to coach us for the university entrance English examination, but she took those marching orders as a prerogative to do for us what she might have done for her own offspring if she had not been a spinster. Several decades before a hip generation discovered what that very proper old maid was teaching us, she tried to prepare us to make four years of college into an experience. It was important to master subjects and pass examinations, she never failed to say, but it was just as important to have fun. It was just as important to converse over coffee, to date, to make friends with students from other places and differing backgrounds, to go to the movies, and to read books picked up only because they looked interesting. As our senior year dragged on into spring and as college beckoned, she made us realize that a higher education would prepare us for careers, but that the most important career of all was living itself.

One day in English class I heard in the lethargy of a warm spring afternoon an unfamiliar word: "anthropology." "Who can tell the class what anthropology is?" she asked. A couple of hands went up. Others stirred at what promised to be a welcome diversion—any diversion was welcome—from diagramming sentence structures. A bad guess up toward the front, and then another. Finally it appeared that not one of us really knew what anthropology was about, and only a couple had the glimmerings of a notion. Then I heard for the first time: anthropology is the science of man. "Don't fail to take it in your freshman year," we were urged. That's what she had done as a major in English literature many years before, and she wanted us to have the same experience, even those of us who talked bravely of pursuing mathematics, physics, or engineering.

Several of us went from that classroom to the University of California, Berkeley, not because it was a great university, but because for us it was the nearest local college. We commuted from home on the streetcar. And not only did most of us pass Subject A, the English test, but we ended up taking the introductory course in anthropology. For me, the theatricality of that introduction has never dimmed. To an impressionable freshman, the enormity of Wheeler Auditorium induced awe. Thirteen hundred of us crowded in, standing along the walls and sitting along the edge of the speaker's platform. At ten after the hour a hush fell over the audience. Up onto the platform and toward the podium, where a microphone was set up, a man walked who seemed the very embodiment of higher learning, tall, gray-moustached Robert H. Lowie. The rumor reached us that he was famous, an internationally known scientist who could lecture gracefully in German or French when the occasion required. In the half-dark hall, well toward the back and off to one side, with a high school crony on either side, I began to learn about anthropology.

Anthropology is the discipline which deals with human biology and the cultures of human groups, we were told. Culture, we rapidly learned, was the key concept, the fundamental principle. Dr. Lowie always spoke very deliberately, taking care to be precise and accurate. "By 'culture,'" he said, "we understand the sum total of what an individual acquires from his society—those beliefs, customs, artistic norms, food habits, and crafts which come to him not by his own creative activity but as a legacy from the past, conveyed by formal or informal education."[1]

True to Lowie's definition, we spent a semester learning about the seemingly endless variety of human customs. We even memorized a small museum. For weeks we made regular visits to the old red brick building where several rooms exhibited a potpourri of artifacts ranging from a gold Mycenaean death mask to obsidian arrowheads an Indian named Ishi once made for shooting game. In a slide quiz we had to be able to identify any object in those rooms, telling what each was, where it came from, how old it was, and how it was used. In discussion group exercises and on written examinations we were forced further to show we were familiar with large parts of the world cultural inventory.

To this day, I find that part of the fun of being an anthropologist is knowing some of the facts of cultural diversity. Beliefs: In a hospital in Australia an aborigine died recently, even though attending physicians could find nothing organically wrong. He had been killed by a sorcerer who magically hurled a finger-length spear at him from a place miles away. Apparently the victim's belief in spiritual weapons was sufficiently great to result in his own demise. Customs: Tuareg men wear veils and consider it indecent to uncover their mouths, even while eating. Tuareg women, however, have no such taboo. Neighboring Muslims also have the custom of the veil, but among them it is the women who conceal their faces and the men who are uncovered. Artistic norms: Bambara antelope carvings in wood can always be recognized because of the characteristic way in which the head and horns are elongated. Similarly with food habits, crafts, or any other cultural category; any anthropologist can go on indefinitely in this vein.

The facts of culture provide a focal subject matter for anthropology, and anthropologists enjoy expert knowledge of cultural variety and complexity. That is a characterization of the field, and even though a concern with cultural facts is not unique to anthropology, it is central to it. Science, however, involves more than the encyclopedic description of a subject. Early work in any field may rely heavily on simple description, but scientific maturity requires emphasis upon a body of theory, upon the search for more or less abstract statements about regularities in the processes of continuity and change. This is true of any science. It is true of anthropology.

To some extent, then, anthropology is distinguished from other fields by its subject matter: human custom. To some extent, it is distinguished by a body of theory. Central to that body of theory has been the concept of culture itself, for while "culture" designates certain descriptive facts, what Clyde Kluckhohn has called "designs for living," it also designates certain regularities about those designs.[2] For Kluckhohn, the regularity is that culture is "historically created." He had in mind the same process as Lowie, who taught us at Berkeley that culture is acquired by an individual from his society through education, by which he meant learning in the broadest sense. Alfred Lewis Kroeber encapsulated the importance of culture as a statement about process when he observed that "perhaps *how it comes to be* is really more distinctive of culture than what it *is*."[3]

Professors Kroeber and Kluckhohn jointly emphasized the significance for anthropology of this concept of culture when they noted that "few intellectuals will challenge the statement that the idea of culture, in the technical anthropological sense, is one of the key notions of contemporary American thought. In explanatory importance and in generality of application it is comparable to such categories as gravity in physics, disease in medicine, evolution in biology."[4] Today, as when I took my introductory course in the subject, the concept of culture is considered central to the discipline. Yet does it give coherence to our research efforts? Does it give integrity to the discipline? I think not.

The concept of culture as a never-ending process of social learning survives as a truism. There was a time when social scientists and humanists needed to be told that human behavior above all is a product of social heredity, of learning, and therefore different from instinctual kinds of activity. The behavior of every society (and every individual) is stimulated and modulated by a culture, a body of tradition. Even those who "do their own thing" do so in terms of conventions accepted by others like themselves. We needed to be told this. We needed to be told that Chinese, Nigerians, or Englishmen differ primarily because they are born into different traditions, rather than because they are biologically (racially) diverse. This has implications for how you deal with people. If human variability is the product of biological differences, then coping with human problems becomes a matter of racial policy or genetic engineering. But since most such variability is the result of learning in a social context, problems that arise must be treated as social and educational ones. This was important to know and still is, but it can be taken now as a given, an assumption which need no longer be argued.

The concept of culture is really a premise, something we assume to be true. But a field of science must be defined as a field of inquiry, not as a statement of what we already know. The organizational concepts must ask questions. The concept of culture has not been a question in most research since the nineteenth century. At that time, while gradually it was becoming clear that human social behavior is largely learned, the idea of culture directed a search to discover the extent to which behavior is learned or instinctual. But by the end of the century, that search was substantially ended. In 1871, Edward Burnett Tylor summarized a conclusion about culture which eventually was accepted everywhere as a statement of what we know, not of a problem to be solved. "Culture or civilization, taken in its wide ethnographic sense," he wrote, "is that complex whole which includes knowledge, belief, art, morals, law, custom, and any other capabilities and habits acquired by man as a member of society."[5]

If the concept of culture does not provide a theoretical orientation for anthropologists, what does? The answer, I believe, is the search for regularities in culture change and continuity. Even in the nineteenth century, when culture emerged as the key principle, the search for an acceptable theory of culture change—phrased as the study of cultural evolution—gave meaning to ethnographic facts. After the turn of the century, a reaction to excesses of imaginative but unscientific interpretation in the reconstruction of evolutionary stages diverted the search for generalizations about culture change. The quest was nearly abandoned in favor of limited efforts to reconstruct the history of particular cultures or culture traits. The term "ethnology," which today designates the anthropologist in his capacity as a student of living peoples, still may be taken to refer more specifically to conclusions drawn in the early decades of the twentieth century about how a culture trait tends to diffuse from tribe to tribe within an environmentally defined culture area. Many anthropologists actually turned their backs on the subject of culture change. Psychological anthropologists in the thirties and forties took an essentially ahistorical approach to study the way in which an individual in childhood internalizes the values, attitudes, and behavioral patterns characteristic of his society. Functionalists at about the same time became almost antihistorical in their focus upon how the various elements of a culture normally fit together to form systemic wholes. Social anthropologists in Britain seemed to dominate the field in the forties and fifties as they turned functional analysis in the direction of highly technical investigations into the way in which kinship systems operate in a given time and place, generally giving no attention to changes of system. Yet a spark of concern with culture change persisted throughout these decades, and it flamed anew in the fifties, sixties, and seventies as a concern of almost every member of the profession.

Today anthropology finds direction in this concern. Although anthropologists, as always, want to know how people live, inevitably now their studies take place against a background of how lives are changing or have changed. The subject of culture change, however, is a quest for knowledge, not a comprehensive body of theory accepted by all. And that is as it should be. To be alive, a science must be organized around the asking of questions and the endless search for uniformities.

Anthropology as a science is distinguished from other sciences in part by (1) its subject matter, the facts of culture. In part it is distinguished by (2) a theoretical orientation, the search for regularities in culture change and continuity. But in part it is also distinguished by (3) its techniques of analysis, the comparative method.

Controlled comparison is a method for discovering cultural regularities. By carefully collecting facts on any topic under study—clothing habits, family organization, religious beliefs, or what have you—the analyst searches for likenesses and differences among various societies. In the study of initiation rites, for example, we have learned that the Plains Indians used to put youths through a coming-of-age ritual in which young men tortured themselves, cutting strips of skin from their arms and legs, chopping off the ends of their fingers, and pulling heavy weights attached to skewers in their skin. The practice in many ways is distinctively Plains Indian, yet many societies initiate youths. Among the Nuer of Africa, boys lie side by side as an elder incises lines on their foreheads, often cutting to the bone. Formerly, Samoan boys, already circumcised, underwent several months of painful tattooing when around sixteen years old. In America, a youth typically undergoes a rite in which he puts on a long, uncomfortable gown, wears a flat cap with a tassel, sits uneasily through seemingly endless speeches, and then marches solemnly up to a representative of the older generation to receive a piece of paper and a handshake.

From looking at societies all over the world we can document a regularity in human behavior: in most societies, young people undergo some kind of initiation. The analyst, of course, attempts to push further. Some reason must lie behind such a widespread practice. Long ago, Arnold Van Gennep suggested one explanation might be that such practices ease the movement of individuals from one status to another as they progress through the life cycle.[6] The initiation of young people, he argued, is a rite of passage which dramatizes and lubricates the transition from child to adult. After his initiation, a youth is more easily regarded and treated by others as a warrior-hunter among the Plains Indians, a warrior-herdsman among the Nuer, an adult worker among the Samoans, and a potential employee or draftee among the Americans.

Differences are as important as similarities. The Lapps of northern Scandinavia do not initiate their young people. This would suggest a hypothesis: the transition from child to adult is not always so dramatic that it evokes the support of a rite of passage. The hypothesis seems to hold. In his work among certain Finnish Lapps, Pertti J. Pelto found, "There are no sharp breaks of any kind in the experience of the individual Skolt as he matures from childhood to adolescence and adulthood. No initiation rites of any important kind take place, and there comes no time when the adults suddenly demand that a child assume full responsibility for adult tasks. . . ."[7]

By comparisons, then, we gradually build up our capacity to generalize about human behavior. As concerns the significance of rites of passage, anthropologists in the tradition of Van Gennep are still exploring, still refining and elaborating on their understanding of the regularities they can identify;[8] and this is just one problem among many.

The comparative method is central to anthropology, yet in basic concept it is so simple and straightforward that thinking men have always employed it. The poet Mark Van Doren describes it as the fundamental technique for understanding people when he says: "There are two statements about human beings that are true: that all human beings are alike, and that all are different. On those two facts all human wisdom is founded." Clearly, the method of comparative analysis does not belong exclusively to anthropologists, but they alone have systematically developed it in a very comprehensive way.

In its distinctively anthropological application, the comparative method is geographically comprehensive. It became clear early that field investigations by trained ethnographers (field workers) provided vastly better descriptive data than the reports of missionaries, traders, and government officials. At first, nearby peoples were studied. In America, Lewis Henry Morgan did intensive work among the Iroquois of New York. In Australia, Lorimer Fison and A. W. Howitt studied the outback Kamileroi and the Kurnai. No such opportunities lay near at hand in England, but improvements in transportation soon made foreign expeditions possible. In 1898, Alfred C. Haddon led a team of scientists to islands in the Torres Straits just off the south coast of New Guinea, and as the twentieth century emerged, ethnologists penetrated remote areas in every corner of the earth, so that now only a few places remain—as in the highlands of New Guinea, the rainforests of Brazil, the hinterlands of Africa, the desert backlands of Eurasia—where unstudied cultures still survive.

The comprehensiveness of the anthropological method means attention to all societies, from the simplest to the most complex. Earlier field work concentrated on the few remaining hunting groups and on people in stateless societies where subsistence was based upon relatively uncomplicated horticultural, pastoral, or fishing techniques. But as the Industrial Revolution gained momentum, the number of such peoples declined rapidly. It became hard to find societies for whom a simpler way of life remained more than a memory. Bronislaw Malinowski pointed this out in 1922 when he published a study of the Trobriand Islanders. "Ethnology is in the sadly ludicrous, not to say tragic, position," he wrote, "that at the very moment when it begins to put its workshop in order, to forge its proper tools, to start ready for work on its appointed task, the material of its study melts away with hopeless rapidity."[9] Anthropologists turned increasingly to the study of more complex societies. It was difficult to use older methods in the study of these societies, however. By their very nature, with pervasive class differences, urban and rural components, regional variations and mutual interdependence, complex societies seemed to defy comprehensive analysis. Yet by the 1940s, the effort was under way, and in our time most field research is concerned with modern nations.

Anthropology is historically comprehensive. The focus on culture change leads many ethnologists to study short-term phenomena because rapid change has come to characterize nearly every society in the world today. But long-term change is not neglected, and anthropologists share with historians an interest in the cultures of earlier centuries. Some anthropologists work with archival, literary, and other documentary sources just as historians do. Others attempt to reconstruct the past by mapping the distribution of culture traits, analyzing languages, interviewing old people, and in other ways drawing inferences from the present about the past. The early concentration on hunters and simple horticulturists reflects this concern with the past, since it was assumed that the early stages in the evolution of human society would be illuminated by learning what we could of contemporaries still relying upon ancient technologies. This interest in the past of man also extends to prehistoric times. Since man as such is several million years old, and since his earliest ancestors are as old as life itself, anthropologists in their guise as paleoanthropologists or archeologists join paleontologists in studying the last 65 million years in particular; and we are willing to look beyond that to the very beginnings of the earth.

The comprehensiveness of anthropology includes a concern with biological as well as cultural problems. In every society, behavior clearly results from an equation which puts the human body up against an inherited tradition, and we want to work with the whole equation. Biological factors affect culture: in Tierra del Fuego, a Yahgan Indian can sleep nearly naked on the freezing ground with no apparent ill effects. Biologically, he is adapted differently from a white man for survival in a cold climate, so culturally he can get along without clothing in that part of the world, at the most protecting himself against the elements by covering himself with grease and throwing a sea skin over his shoulders. To live in such a cold region, a white man must have a culture which includes some form of warm clothing and substantial housing.

Cultural factors also affect the body and body functioning. I have in my office the skull of a California Indian. From an examination of various cranial characteristics I estimate it to be that of a woman who died in the last century while still young, perhaps 20 years of age. Yet the teeth, though healthy, are worn to the gumline, and in that way are very unlike the teeth of her descendants still living in California. Cultural factors are the reason. Aboriginal Californians regularly ate acorn porridge containing enough abrasive material to grind the teeth down rather fast. The consequences for their health were serious, since they had no prosthetic dentures. Modern Californians, Indian or white, eat food which may cause caries and lead to early tooth loss—culture still affects dentition and mastication—but modern culture includes dental treatment which can alleviate or solve the health problem. Because biological and cultural phenomena are related in many ways, we include both in our perspective on man.

Finally, anthropology is holistic; rather than limiting himself to art, or technology, or some other discrete subject, the anthropologist tries to comprehend them all. In Dr. Lowie's course we learned about techniques of hunting, fishing, farming, and herding, but also about fire, cooking, and meals, dress and ornament, houses and settlements, handicrafts, trade and transportation, amusements, art, war, marriage and the family, the clan, rank, etiquette, property, government and law, religion and magic, knowledge and science, and language.[10] Early anthropologists were especially remarkable for the extent to which they were able to gather information on so wide a range of topics. Perhaps because they often found themselves in very remote places where the remnants of an old tribe were living out their last years, ethnographers tried to record what they could about everything while they had the chance, moving with apparent ease from collecting folk tales and working out genealogies to sketching architecture or recording music.

The attempt to record everything found expression in theorizing. Ethnologists, with their interest in historical reconstructions, attempted to make cultural inventories in terms of traits and complexes, worrying over whether the bow and arrow are one trait or several (that is, bow, arrow shaft, and flaked stone point), or whether the lasso is better regarded as a culture trait in itself or as part of a complex which, with horse, saddle, stirrups, and bridle, spread widely among the American Indians after the Spanish conquest. Functionalists for 40 years devoted themselves to the search for a model to depict the ways in which all the elements of a culture hold together. It started with Malinowski's 1922 analysis of ritual trade among the Trobriand Islanders.[11] He found that the ceremonial exchange of non-utilitarian bracelets and necklaces could be seen as related to nearly everything the Trobrianders did, since it had economic implications, affected status and prestige, was embroidered with religious beliefs and practices, and expressed values and attitudes. Eventually much functional analysis dealt only with social organization, but it began with a holistic orientation and always remained holistic in principle.

As used in anthropology, then, the comparative method is very comprehensive. It covers the globe geographically, ranges from the smallest and simplest to the largest and most complex of societies, stretches historically into the farthest reaches of the past, ventures beyond the social sciences and humanities to stake claims in the territory of biological sciences, and is so holistic it excludes no category of human behavior from its realm. It may reasonably be observed that a discipline which attempts so much takes the risk of not being a discipline at all; technically sophisticated research melts into dilettantism if one attempts to do too many things. And, indeed, within anthropology one encounters a strong tendency for investigators to restrict their work to sharply delimited problems. The history of anthropology, as often happens in the careers of individual anthropologists, is one of a ceaseless give-and-take between narrowly restricted, rather technical kinds of research and the broadest of interpretive writing. This is as true today as it was in the past. However, the field still belongs to the champions of a comprehensive discipline.

Anthropology is the study of man, Dr. Lowie told us on our first day of class, but neither he nor any other anthropologist would claim a monopoly on that subject. Scholars in many different disciplines study man. Each discipline is distinctive, however, in the way pertinent data are identified, the problems that are tackled, and the analytical methods that are used. Anthropology is distinguished by its reliance upon the comparative method to search for regularities about the processes of change and continuity in cultures from every time and place.

An approach which is so global in subject matter, so wide-ranging in its interest, which uses the method on which "all human wisdom is founded," offers more than a profession to an anthropologist; it offers a world view which gives meaning to everything he sees and does. And it is this perspective on the world and all the people in it that the student, young or old, gets from his training in anthropology. It was for this reason that Dr. Lowie had us memorize a museum, and it was for this reason that my English teacher urged us all to take a course in anthropology. Even for those who do not go on to take more advanced courses, who do not seek a career in this discipline, knowledge of anthropology has a place because it helps equip one to succeed in the most important career of all, which is living itself.

# 2　The Garden of Eden

Where was the Garden of Eden? When was it? These questions have long puzzled men, quite independently of theological dogma and Bishop Ussher's pronouncement that Adam was created in 4004 B.C. Eugène DuBois's discovery of the remains of Java man (*Homo erectus*) in 1891 seemed to confirm an old notion that man first emerged from his shadowy past somewhere in the East. If not the biblical Garden of Eden, then at least an early evolutionary breeding ground appeared to have been discovered in Asia.

A few decades later, in 1924, Raymond Dart found the first remains of the man-ape (*Australopithecus*) in South Africa; and as the significance of this and corroborative finds grew upon us during the next several decades, it seemed the place of man's origin was not the East after all, but Africa, perhaps 2 million years ago. Today, many argue that man first appeared in Africa, but the topic is complicated, and the first requirement in broaching it is to examine the context of time.

A distinguished historian occupies the office across from mine here at Mills College. He is absorbed just now with writing the biography of a famous American. His work would be impossible without a calendar. Imagine attempting to describe the life of an individual without being able to establish clearly and with some precision what the sequence of events was. Sometimes even a calendar is not sufficiently precise, and a clock is needed. When dive bombers and torpedo planes unleashed their fury over Honolulu on December 7, 1941, it was significant that the time was 7:35 on a Sunday morning, a time when most of the individuals whose lives were affected were still in bed rather than at their posts.

When the subject is man's prehistoric ancestry, then the problem is not that measures need to be more precise, but something of the opposite. Just as it would be cumbersome on the whole to chronicle the significant events of a man's life in hours, minutes, and seconds rather than in days and years, it would be cumbersome to talk about prehistoric events in terms of years and centuries because the time spans involved are very long. In part for this reason, and in part because our measuring instruments do not always allow us to be precise in terms of years and centuries, we relate developments in human antiquity to the sequential phases of a geological calendar.

Geological time reckoning is not based upon periodic movements of the sun, but on major changes in the ecology of the earth (topography, weather, flora, and fauna) as we know of these through the research of geologists and paleontologists. From such a calendar we see that man is not merely December's child; he is a child of the late evening of December 31, a Christmas present that came late and may yet be exchanged.

More precisely, the earth appears now to be about 5 billion years old. From the perspective of man, that is an enormous length of time. Yet for approximately the first 4 billion, 400 million years, the so-called Pre-Cambrian period, the highest form of life to emerge was no more complex than such fauna as worms and radiolaria or such flora as algae. Imagine the earth so inhabited, and the grandeur of our planet today can better be appreciated.

For approximately the first 2 billion years, designated as the Azoic era, the earth supported no life at all. It was a chemical no-man's-land. For approximately the next 2 billion years, the Archeozoic era, the first stirrings of life appeared in the shape of microscopic one-celled beings (protozoa). Only in the last 400 million years or so of the Pre-Cambrian period, the Proterozoic era, did simple multicelled (metazoan) creatures evolve.

The history of complex plants and animals, then, is crowded into the last 600 million years of a very old planet. During this length of time, three eras succeeded one another, each dramatically different from the next in the life forms it supported. The Paleozoic era is the first of these three. (Because its earliest subdivision is the Cambrian period, the three earlier eras are referred to collectively as Pre-Cambrian.) The Paleozoic era lasted about 400 million years, and while its most obvious feature was the appearance of vertebrates and a great proliferation of fish—its Devonian period is known as the Age of Fishes—comparatively minor developments had special significance for man. For the first time in any detectable way, living things left the sea which was their womb. Land plants appeared, followed some millions of years later by the first land animals, ancestors of today's frogs, newts, and salamanders which were born in the water but spent their adult lives out of it (amphibians). A few more million years later, and not only had the first winged insects appeared, but primitive reptiles evolved out of amphibians to diversify into numerous kinds by the end of the era, presaging a new age.

Lasting roughly from 200 million years to 65 million years ago, the Mesozoic era was the Age of Dinosaurs (giant reptiles). A description of the great seas and swamps that covered the earth then, and of the largest animals that have ever lived, provides exciting fare for any adventurer in the world of science. Not only did reptiles in many shapes and sizes appear, but so too did the first birds and more advanced forms of plant life. Most directly significant for man, however, was the appearance of primitive mammals, small, rare additions to a landscape in which at first they would have scarcely been noticed. By the end of the era, mammals largely had replaced reptiles as dominant figures in the world animal census. It is they who stand out in the most recent era, the Cenozoic.

The Cenozoic, approximately the last 65 million years, is a rather short length of time in geochronological perspective, yet it is the time when man's ancestors underwent the long, gradual process of separation from other warm-blooded, suckling mammals. Fully developed man appeared only at the very end of this era. Even so, the whole 65 million years is especially important to know about. Today we face nearly overwhelming problems of human adjustment in a world suddenly grown small and insecure. Attempts to solve these problems must take into account the nature of man—the extent to which he is just another kind of animal, but also the extent to which he is uniquely human. To ascertain what the nature of man is, it is essential to learn how, during the course of the Cenozoic, he got to be what he is. Yet where is the evidence for such a perspective? How can we know about events which took place millions of years before any man was around to make records?

The taxonomic method pioneered by Linnaeus in the eighteenth century offers a first step toward unveiling man's evolutionary progress. The method is simple. Animals are compared for similarities and differences. If two or more animals are anatomically nearly identical, they can be regarded as belonging to a single species or variety of a species. With lesser similarity they are categorized as members of a single genus, family, order, class, or phylum. Since similarities are presumed to be the result of common ancestry, such a classification amounts to an abbreviated statement of history indicating biological ties of relationship.

Applying the method to living animals, we can conclude that the chimpanzee is the closest relative of man still alive, even though a very long period of time must separate chimp and man from their common apelike ancestor. Monkeys must represent more distant relatives. But we must take care not to repeat a common error in this regard. Laymen generally neglect to take into account the likelihood that just as man has changed since he branched off from subhuman ancestors, so too have all other living relatives. The common ancestor of both ape and man, or monkey and man, need not—in fact could not—have had many of the characteristics of living apes or monkeys. Certainly the ability of South American monkeys to hang by their tails appeared after the two families had already separated, and that is only a most obvious example.

The point is this: the kinship of man with living monkeys and apes does not imply that early ancestors of man looked and acted exactly like present-day descendants. Just what such ancestors were like must remain speculative insofar as we rely solely upon our knowledge of living creatures. Even so, recent work in the taxonomic tradition allows us to say this much about our kinship with other living animals: we can draw convincing conclusions about which are closest to man in ancestry, and we can estimate how much time has passed since they and man diverged from their common parents.

As long as gross anatomical comparisons were relied upon, only rough guesses could be made about the closeness of man to other living animals. Turning to blood chemistry, however, added new possibilities for precision. One line of research grew out of familiarity with the way in which the body fights disease.

When a so-called antigen gets into an animal's bloodstream as some form of invading bacteria, virus, or other protein substance, a biochemical reaction takes place. Antibodies are produced which have the power to neutralize or destroy the antigen. Immunization against disease takes advantage of this fact. Through inoculation, a weakened form of the bacteria or virus, the vaccine, is introduced into the body. Once in the bloodstream it stimulates the production of antibodies which can then ward off the antigen if it attacks. From this knowledge a test was devised to measure the relationship of one species of animal to another.

In an early, simple form of this test, human serum, a protein substance, was injected into a rabbit. Later, the blood of that rabbit was drawn off and the serum separated. The rabbit blood had developed antibodies hostile to human serum, so when the antihuman rabbit serum was mixed with the blood of a human being it showed its hostility by producing a heavy precipitation. This antihuman serum, then, could be used to determine whether or not a given blood sample was human. If added, for example, to horse blood, it produced no precipitation at all.

At this point, something provocative for evolutionary research was done. Antihuman serum was added to chimpanzee blood. It did not produce the complete precipitation normally produced with human blood, but it did generate about 85 percent of that precipitation. The chimpanzee appears, by this measure as by others, to be closely related to man. Monkey blood also showed some precipitation, although not much. The monkey seems a more distant relative, yet far closer than the dog, whose blood showed no precipitation at all.

At the University of California, Berkeley, Vincent M. Sarich worked out a much more refined version of this test, one capable of giving readings where earlier efforts showed nothing. From this work he confirmed biochemically what grosser anatomical comparisons suggested.[1] Our closest living relatives appear to be the apes—chimpanzees, gorillas, orangutans, and gibbons. Our next closest relatives seem to be Old World monkeys, then New World monkeys, and most distantly within the category of man and his animal relatives (the order of Primates), the so-called prosimians, animals such as the tarsier, lemur, and tree shrew.

On the whole, this immunological work substantiates what we had thought concerning man's closeness to other Primates, and is valuable for increasing our capacity to be precise in this regard. In addition, the biochemical difference between any two animals is taken as a measure of time elapsed since separation of the two from their common ancestor. By this measure, man apparently diverged from the chimp-gorilla line approximately 3.5 million years ago ($\pm$ 1.5 million), while the man and ape line separated from the stock of Old World monkeys around 22 million years ago ($\pm$ 2 million). These dates seem much too recent, however, and since the inference is based upon unproven assumptions about the regularity of molecular evolution (in this case, albumin macromolecules in the blood), such dates can only be taken as suggestive. Even so, they add to our sense of how man became what he is.

Taxonomic analysis yields important clues to the evolution of man. But they are only clues, since the evidence is indirect. We can infer relationships with a good deal of confidence. We can infer time of separation, even though this assumes a consistency in the rate of evolutionary development which cannot be proved. We can even make some inferences about the nature of early forms, such as that the common ancestor of monkeys, apes, and man did not have a prehensile tail. All of this is valuable to know, but it is only what in a court of law would be termed circumstantial evidence. It is very compelling on some points and merely suggestive on others, but in all cases it falls short of constituting direct proof. Fortunately, we also have access to a large and growing body of facts which constitute empirical evidence for the evolution of man from subhuman forms. We have the fossil remains of Primates that lived at various times far in the past.

The fossil record provides direct evidence for ancestral forms of life, but it is not easy to make use of it. Our research is far from finished, and there are still many gaps in the data, with many questions still unanswered, for while a lot of digging has been done, a lot still remains. This problem of gaps is serious. It costs a lot of money to finance an expedition, so only a small part of the exploration that ought to be done has yet been accomplished, even though we have been at the job for over 100 years. Further, the amount of information we want is large. Ideally, we should have sample whole skeletons from the wide-ranging populations of innumerable species of Primates for each of a tremendously long sequence of time periods.

Unfortunately, many skeletons have undoubtedly not survived to be recovered, even if we had the manpower with which to go after them. Like other creatures, Primates normally end up being eaten and digested, their bones gnawed, cracked, and broken. If skeletal materials survive the violence of death, they still have only a small chance of enduring for more than a century or two. Surface material usually disintegrates with weathering. It has a better chance if, by rare accident, it somehow gets covered with earth. Dry earth may preserve it forever. Most commonly, soil is wet, at least from time to time, and then the soil chemistry is significant. If subsoil water is high in mineral content, water-soaked bone cells may be replaced with inorganic molecules to form a highly durable material. More commonly, mild acidity in the soil causes bones to disappear without detectable trace. Sometimes bones end up in swamps or lakes, where they generally disintegrate, but where mineralization also is possible. Similarly, carnivores may drag them into caves where dampness may destroy, but where sometimes extreme dryness or mineralization can preserve. The result is that, of the myriad of individuals that have lived and died, only a tiny fraction survive to be found by paleoanthropologists.

Because the evidence is incomplete, discussion of it can easily bog down in technical digressions about how one particular find relates to another. To make sense of these data as a total record, we need to leave aside such diversions in favor of a larger perspective. As concerns the time dimension, it is useful to work in terms of the six epochs which succeeded one another as geochronological subdivisions of the Cenozoic: Paleocene, Eocene, Oligocene, Miocene, Pliocene, and Pleistocene. Each was millions of years in length, long enough for a multitude of evolutionary changes to take place. Yet the measure of an epoch is precise enough for our purposes.

In addition, it helps to work in terms of grades—levels of development—rather than of individual skeletal finds as such. More often than not, the fossil record does not include specimens directly descended the one from the other. Rather, it is as though a million years from now an investigator wanted to talk about the twentieth century ancestor of an evolved form of Colobus monkey when his only skeletal remains might be those of a baboon, half a dozen Rhesus macaques, and the teeth of a guenon monkey. That man of tomorrow would not be able to state precisely what the Colobus ancestor was like. But he would be able to speak of the general level of development, the grade, of monkeys which lived at that time in the past. This, in effect, is what I will be doing as I attempt to talk about the antecedents of man as we know of them today, when our evidence is incomplete, much less complete than we reasonably can hope for it to be even a decade or two from now. It will never be perfect, but it has been improving, and hopefully will continue to become more complete. For an overview of what we know now, however, we will succeed best if the terms of discussion are taken to be that Primate form most like man in each epoch.[2]

Beginning with the Paleocene (about 65 million years ago), the highest grade was that which can be designated primitive prosimian. In both hemispheres, the remains of small arboreal mammals have been found which have been designated the Plesiadapidae (genus *Plesiadapis*). Ranging from the size of mice to that of house cats, they resembled in some details of skeletal anatomy the lemurs of a later time. But lemur resemblances were so slight that they scarcely distinguished them from some of their own contemporaries which were ancestral rodents and insectivores.

Living tree shrews appear to be relatively unchanged descendants of Paleocene prosimians. Not much about them suggests the order of Primates. Yet, as compared with other small, insect-eating mammals, they have slightly larger brains and their eyesight is somewhat more developed, at the expense of their sense of smell. They use their paws awkwardly to handle objects, and one extinct form had fingernails, a uniquely Primate feature associated with manual dexterity.

Prosimians higher than tree shrews—monkeys, apes, and man—are presumably the much evolved descendants of this same basic stock. Because of gaps in the record, however, it is not possible at this time to demonstrate a direct sequence from one of the Plesiadapidae to any of the higher Primates. This is why it is useful to talk in terms of grades. During the Paleocene, early Primates began to diverge from other mammals. We cannot be sure we have specimens from the actual ancestral stock of man. But we can assume that however different in details, this earliest Primate ancestor must have been similar in general type to the Plesiadapidae, the best known members of a grade characterized by some slight enlargement of the brain, an improvement in eyesight, and a tendency to use the paws as primitive hands, but a grade otherwise small and undistinguished.

While some early Primates became extinct or persisted relatively without change up to the present, others by Eocene times had evolved into two familiar kinds of Primate, lemurs and tarsiers, precocious members of the grade prosimian.

During the Eocene (*circa* 40 to 65 million years ago), archaic lemurs became abundant all over the northern part of what then was an American-European continent. One of the American lemurs, for example, was *Smilodectes,* a small creature still showing his Paleocene ancestry, but with eyes now shifted to the front to give better depth perception, a very useful ability for tree-dwelling animals. Growing intelligence is seen too in the relative enlargement of the frontal part of the brain.

Lemurs became nearly extinct at the end of the Eocene, but some survived to the present on Madagascar, where they have been available for study. Although no longer identical with Eocene forebears, the basic skeletal resemblance is strong, suggesting that the behavior of living lemurs still resembles that of *Smilodectes* and other Eocene forms, at least generically. Depth (stereoscopic) vision and a reduced sense of smell (as compared with tree shrews and other primitive prosimians) are confirmed. A growing capacity to manipulate objects with hands is indicated skeletally. They have thumbs rotated to face the other fingers (opposable thumbs) and fingernails, both of which improve the capacity to pick things up. Living lemurs, however, seldom use the opposable thumb for carrying food to their mouths. Like quadrupeds, they hold food down with their paws and bring their mouths to the food. The mouth itself has not yet become distinctively Primate. Lemurs have long, projecting snouts with moist muzzles (the rhinarium), split upper lips, and tactile whiskers. Higher Primates, in contrast, have flexible lips, dry skin around the nostrils, and a development of the muscles which allows them to make faces.

Lemurs were not the highest form of Primate in the Eocene, since tarsiers also appeared at that time throughout the northern part of the giant continent. Anatomically, the latter had evolved to a level somewhere between lemurs and monkeys. The tarsier brain case is relatively larger, and the development of eyesight proceeded further. Their eyesight did not become more stereoscopic, since lemurs already were completely developed in their capacity for depth perception. But the eye got better bony protection as the orbit in which the eye rests assumed the developed primate characteristic of being completely enclosed at the sides and the back.

Tarsiers, like lemurs, became nearly extinct after a period in the Eocene when they thrived. Fortunately, some survived on islands in the Malay Archipelago where we can see them today, still similar to their ancient predecessors. Behaviorally, perhaps the most distinctive advance over lower prosimians was that they could make faces. Tarsiers have free upper lips and dry noses. Such differences, however, do not separate them greatly from lemurs, and the grade prosimian remained one characterized essentially by relative advancement in brain size, visual acuity, and manual ability, with just the beginnings of facial flexibility.

The end of the Eocene was also the end of prosimian success. During the Oligocene (circa 28 to 40 million years ago), these animals declined in number until they nearly became extinct. In part, they may have succumbed to the competition of evolving carnivores and rodents, but in part, their niches in the environment appear to have been taken over by more evolved Primates, the grade pithecine. The term suggests itself because, in Greek, pithēkos means either monkey or ape, freeing one from the necessity of deciding whether the creature in question is one or the other. That suits our needs for the Oligocene.

As is clear from the observation of living animals, even within the confines of a zoo, monkeys and apes are not greatly different from one another. Anatomically, the key differences in evolutionary terms are those which distinguish tree-dwelling animals, which mainly move on all fours, from those, also arboreal, which swing by their arms (brachiate) or walk quadrupedally, but on the knuckles of their hands, occasionally rising to two legs momentarily.

Skeletally, these differences in characteristic mode of locomotion are associated with a difference in the placement of the shoulder blades (scapulae), which in apes are located across the back instead of on the sides of the rib cage, freeing the arms to reach high with ease. They are also associated with differences in the number of vertebrae in the lower back (lumbar) region; apes and men have shorter, stiffer backs than monkeys, apes generally only having three lumbar vertebrae, men five, but monkeys six or seven. Additionally, monkeys have tails, helping four-footed animals maintain balance, but hindering those who swing by their arms.

We have the partial remains of a number of Oligocene Primates from the Old World. (Very few Oligocene sites have been found so far. The best is in the Fayum Depression of Egypt.) Unfortunately, they consist mostly of teeth, which tell us nothing of the location of the shoulder bones, the number of lower vertebrae, or the presence of a tail. This is not the only instance in which our data are mostly dental; teeth are the hardest part of the body, so we often find only teeth to go by. Fortunately, one can infer a great deal about an animal from its teeth. Just compare the teeth of a dog with those of a horse or a cow, and you will see how clearly dentition reflects basic dietary habits.

Teeth differences between monkeys and apes, presumably reflecting differences in eating habits, are as striking as those of the postcranial skeleton. Monkeys have teeth with the so-called bilophodont pattern; that is, the molars have ridges along the inner and outer edges of the top of the tooth which connect each front cusp with the one behind it. Apes have the Y-5 pattern; that is, molars in which a deep crevice separates five cusps to give the shape of a winged Y when looked at from above. Unfortunately, these differences in tooth form do not appear until the next epoch, at least as far as we know today. It is quite conceivable that Oligocene Primates could have been clearly ape in other ways without yet showing the Y-5 pattern, or clearly monkey in other ways without yet evincing the bilophodont pattern.

If all of this seems confusing, it should not be allowed to conceal the fact that we do have considerable evidence for a kind of small, generic monkey-ape type. The evidence includes *Parapithecus,* whose tooth count suggests he probably was a progressive tarsioid or lemuroid. It includes *Amphipithecus* and *Oligopithecus,* which may well be ancestors of Old World monkeys. It includes the remains of *Apidium,* who looks like an ancestor of *Oreopithecus,* a progressive Pliocene ape which became extinct before our time. It seems possible that in *Aeolopithecus* and *Propliopithecus* we have the Oligocene ancestors or ancestor-cousins of the most monkey-like of today's apes, the gibbon. Finally, *Aegyptopithecus,* insofar as we can recognize him from a few teeth and three jaw fragments, may be the ancestor of twentieth century gorillas and chimpanzees.

So what was the grade pithecine? We can speculate. It probably consisted of animals smarter than prosimians, with excellent eyesight, and able, like today's monkeys and apes, to pick up and manipulate things, including food conveyed to the mouth. No doubt, too, they had rather flexible faces, capable of signaling alarm or friendliness or other states of mind as an increment to the general mammal ability to convey emotions through sound and agitation.

The Miocene (*circa* 12 to 28 million years ago) was the epoch of apes. This was not so for the New World, where no higher form evolved out of the grade pithecine, and where man did not appear until he wandered in, fully formed, from Asia at a much later date. But it was so in the Old World, from China to Europe to Africa, where a grade dryopithecine can be identified. Throughout this vast area, apes flourished. Some seem part of the gibbon line, apparently having gone their own way since the Oligocene. Most seem more or less to have been in the line which led in part to modern gorillas, chimpanzees, and orangutans. We already know of between 20 and 30 different genera of this sort, all members of the subfamily dryopithecine. (Some would argue that many of these vary as species rather than genera.) Once again, almost all of our evidence is dental. These apes, like modern great apes (gorillas, chimpanzees, and orangutans), had molars with the Y-5 pattern of cusp and fissure formation. Probably they were somewhat similar to modern great apes, ranging in size from that of large monkeys to gorillas. The few limb bones we have do not suggest animals which habitually swung from limbs or normally walked erect, but we have so few such bones that a clear determination cannot be made at this time.

The grade dryopithecine must remain for the present a rather ill-defined category of ape. This is unfortunate, since one of the dryopithecine species undoubtedly was the apelike ancestor of man. Man and the dryopithecinae both have the Y-5 pattern of cusp formation on their molars, although some living men show a Y-4 variation on the rearmost teeth, where they often have only four cusps. Since only man, these apes, and later apes have this characteristic, and since teeth modify only reluctantly, even this evidence provides a good inferential basis for regarding man as evolved from some line in the grade dryopithecine.

Dryopithecine apes continued to flourish in the Pliocene (*circa* 3 to 12 million years ago), but one form evolved into what is now widely considered the first true man (hominid), *Ramapithecus.* Because very few fragments of *Ramapithecus* have been found so far, he must be categorized primarily in terms of dental remains. From these it appears that his face was more vertical than that of apes, with smaller canine teeth and a mouth which, in the placement of teeth, was wider at the back than at the front. All of these were distinct developments in the human direction.

These cranial features provide reasons for thinking that *Ramapithecus* walked upright. Man, with his small teeth and jaw muscles, has to use his hands and knives, axes, hammers, or other implements as substitute for the sharp, projecting canine teeth and powerful bite his dryopithecine relatives generally possessed. But for hands to be used so extensively for food getting and defense, they needed to be freed from carrying the body. It seems likely that upright posture grew in association with a greater use of the hands, the invention of tools, and the reduction of facial prognathism and canine projection. Hence the facial characteristics of *Ramapithecus* suggest bipedalism. We await confirmation from postcranial finds. Tentatively, however, we can define the highest Pliocene form as the grade ramapithecine, a small creature no larger than a spider monkey or a gibbon, who probably walked upright and relied on his hands and tool-like objects instead of his teeth to stay alive.

The Pleistocene (*circa* the last 3 million years) is preeminently the age of hominids. Because the Pleistocene is so significant for man, even though it started only around 3 million years ago, we need to break it down into smaller calendrical units. Dramatic changes in climate, associated with great changes in the character of plant and animal life, provide the measure of passing time.[3]

The very warm Pliocene cooled to a moist, warm to temperate climate which favored a characteristic kind of animal life found widely in Europe and North America and known as the Villafranchian assemblage. The assemblage included advanced forms of elephants, horses, cattle, and camels. After a time, the ecological characteristics of the Villafranchian yielded to severe geological and climatic alterations. Mountains formed or grew larger and volcanoes erupted. The sea level rose and fell. At times the temperature dropped low enough for large mountain glaciers to form, the last, most severe temperature drop being the Günz glaciation, followed by a warmer period commonly referred to as the First Interglacial. Thus, although the Lower Pleistocene had times of severe cold, it was an introduction to the Ice Age rather than a full expression of it.

The Middle Pleistocene began with the first continental icecap, the Mindel, an enormous glacier which hung heavy over the northern part of the globe, including some northernmost land areas. It gave way, however, to the longest of the interglacial periods, the Second Interglacial, over half a million years of relative warmth and quiet. The Middle Pleistocene was primarily a time when warm weather animals flourished, including new forms of elephants, rhinoceroses, and hippopotamuses. For over half a million years, the warm weather held.

But the Ice Age was not over, for the deep cold of the Riss glaciation gradually established its presence, ushering in the Upper Pleistocene, named the Reindeer Age by French paleoanthropologists. Hippopotamuses disappeared. Cold-adapted mammoths and woolly rhinoceroses replaced their warm-adapted ancestors. Arctic animals flourished, including reindeer, musk-oxen, gluttons, blue foxes, and lemmings. The Third Interglacial intervened, bringing warmth again for a time. Then it gave place to the advances and retreats of the last great icecap, the Würm. It has been about 11,000 years since the end of the main advance of the Würm. It is quite possible that these last years represent the early part of an interglacial period, a continuing phase of the Pleistocene, rather than a new epoch (termed the Holocene). As interglacial periods go, 11,000 years is a very short time.

From the North Pole, icecaps spread over the northern parts of Eurasia and America like three advances and recessions of the tide on a beach. Although the actual movements of ice were complicated, involving numerous advances and retreats within the three larger stages, rough worldwide correlations have been established which are useful for dating the progress of man. The major glaciations of Eurasia, named after sites studied in Europe, correspond to similar glaciations on the American continent. The ice never covered more than the most northerly parts of the continent, except for mountaintops farther south. Most of the land mass remained free of ice, though it became tundralike during glacial periods throughout what now are Europe, America, and mainland Asia. Farther south, including major parts of Africa and Southeast Asia, northern cold periods appear to have been associated with very wet but relatively warm climates in which life could flourish. These so-called pluvial periods provide calendrical markers which can be more or less correlated with glacial movements and tundra conditions in the north.

Ecological fluctuations in the Pleistocene appear to have hastened the evolution of mammals. The pace of human development accelerated. With relative rapidity man evolved from the grade ramapithecine to what he is today. It is useful to identify four Pleistocene grades, of which the earliest is australopithecine, Lower Pleistocene man.[4] The evidence for all four grades is vastly better than for any previous epoch, even though significant gaps still exist. As concerns the Australopithecinae, the remains of scores of individuals are now in our hands, including fragments from most parts of the body.[5] Further, since some of the finds are from caves, we have valuable if incomplete evidence on the food they ate and the objects they used.

A trend perceptible for over 60 million years is visible in the grade australopithecine. The brain continued to enlarge. In absolute figures, the cranial capacity ranged from 435 c.c. in *Australopithecus africanus* to 700 in the related form *Australopithecus robustus.* Living gorillas vary within the same limits, from adult females at 420 c.c. to large males at 752.[6] Gorillas, however, are larger in body size than the old man-apes were. *Australopithecus* was scarcely bigger than *Ramapithecus,* males weighing perhaps 100 pounds when fully grown. If brain size is correlated with body weight, the relative size of the brain is found to be greatly larger than that of any known ape. *Australopithecus* on these grounds would seem a very good candidate for an ancestor of man, in grade if not in direct antecedence.

Excellent evidence that *Australopithecus* walked upright also suggests that he was an ancestor of man. Certain features of the head suggest bipedalism, including the central location of the place where the spinal column attaches, and the low position of the rough area where muscles attach to connect the back of the head to the neck. It appears that his head was balanced on an upright spine. But in addition, the bones of the hip leave no doubt of posture. They are very much like those of modern man, and to that extent very different from those of apes and monkeys. *Australopithecus* without question was an upright walker.

The humanness of Lower Pleistocene man cannot be settled solely on anatomical grounds. Physical development was gradual over time, and it is arbitrary to say that a creature such as *Australopithecus,* who physically was intermediate between men and apes, was a primitive man rather than a precocious ape. Other criteria do not greatly help. *Australopithecus* stands also intermediate in his use of tools. He was a cultured animal, but his culture was very primitive.

The earliest evidence for Primate culture must remain entirely inferential. It seems very likely that the dryopithecine grade had what can be termed a protocultural level of tool use. Miocene apes left no tool remains for analysis. But it is possible they used objects more or less the way living chimpanzees occasionally do. Jane Van Lawick-Goodall, in her field studies in East Africa, has recorded several instances.[7] A thirsty individual unable to reach water cradled in the bole of a tree chewed a wad of leaves which he then used as a sponge. Rather simple, yet it is tool use.

When the termite season appears, chimps use an ingenious technique to get at the tasty delicacy. A stick is selected for proper length and thickness. Cleared of leaves and twigs, it is inserted into the termite nest so that when withdrawn it will have some insects clinging to it which can be licked off by the apparently delighted gourmet. Infants seem to learn from their elders that this is the way it is done. Baboons, who also appear to enjoy the flavor of termites, and who sometimes watch chimps at their work, are totally unable to emulate the practice. It appears to be an achievement of the dryopithecine grade too complex for mastery by lower Primates.

It is unfortunate that we have no information about the cultural habits of *Ramapithecus.* Judging from the australopithecines who succeeded him, however, he could not have been much more advanced than his own antecedents.

And that brings us to *Australopithecus*. His culture can be said to introduce the Old Stone Age, the Paleolithic. But if it is meaningful to regard it as Stone Age in character, it is also meaningful to call it extremely primitive. It is better thought of as Proto-Paleolithic. Australopithecines apparently still had not progressed much beyond the ape's capacity simply to use in a culturally determined way what might be at hand. Raymond Dart has described their tool inventory as a bone-tooth-and-horn industry (osteodontokeratic).[8] It consisted of the leg bones of large animals which served as hammers, jawbones used as knives and saws, jagged pieces of broken long bones which served as daggers and scrapers, and in general, parts of bones, teeth, and horns which could have been used without the need to shape them consciously for their intended purpose. The remains of a meal provided a kit of implements.

Stone tools known as Oldowan (alternatively, pebble or chopper-chopping) tools probably served their needs in scraping a tree limb or butchering an occasional small animal. These tools were manufactured. A few flakes at one end of a piece of stone were struck off in order to give a cutting edge. Not very impressive technologically, such tools represent man's early success in making as opposed merely to using tools. *Australopithecus* appears to have been a hominid in his capacity for technological development as well as in his anatomical status, but his place among the Hominidae must be regarded as very low.

If we take *Ramapithecus* and *Australopithecus* as the two earliest forms of man, where, then, was the Garden of Eden? Many would say it was in Africa. Elwyn L. Simons disagrees, however, and I find his argument compelling.[9] We tend to assume that man had to appear first in a rather delimited area, in part perhaps because we have inherited an old scholarly and biblical tradition of a primeval garden, but also because it is easy to fall into the error of assuming that the earliest known example of a given species is evidence for the place where the new form first appeared. Yet the very search for a circumscribed area such as Africa or Asia is misconceived.

From what we know of evolutionary processes, we would expect the small increments of evolutionary development to occur as part of a process affecting a species throughout its entire range. For species which cover a lot of territory, this is then a wide-ranging process. The range of many species of mammals during the Miocene and Pliocene extended over large parts of Africa and Eurasia. In addition to insectivores, rodents, ruminants, mastondonts, and other kinds of mammals, some Primates had this sort of Old World range, including species of dryopithecine, ramapithecine, and australopithecine. The major finds concerning *Ramapithecus,* in fact, are from northern India and East Africa. The first australopithecine finds were made in South Africa, but in more recent years examples have also turned up in far distant places, including North Africa, East Africa, the eastern Mediterranean, northern China, and Southeast Asia.

From these observations, Simons concludes that "if reports as to localities of *Australopithecus* by several serious students be accepted, the data now show that this earliest generally accepted antecedent of man was widely distributed in tropical regions of the Old World in the early Pleistocene."[10] Man evolved, it appears, as a species-wide development which covered major parts of Africa and Eurasia. No one locality within that range can be said to constitute the place where some dramatic mutation first made an advanced ape into a primitive man. The process was cumulative over a long period of time, and it probably covered much of the Old World.

# 3

# The Real Adam

I remember having seen a television program in which the entertainment focused upon three individuals, each of whom claimed to be a certain person, someone such as Mr. John Doe, the first man to climb Mt. Something-or-other. A panel of judges was allowed to ask questions, but eventually each judge had to state his conclusion as to which of the three truly was the person they all claimed to be, and which were the imposters. After a suitable pause for a commercial, the climax came when the moderator requested, "Will the real John Doe please stand up?" With that, the audience learned who actually was the man they all claimed to be. My remembrance of this program quickened as I was thinking about the question of who the first real man might have been. We have a number of candidates with a claim to being the true Adam, and of the evidence we have, we need to be able to ask, "Will the real Adam please stand up?"

Anthropologists speak of *Australopithecus* as unquestionably a true man (hominid), and most agree that when we get more information on *Ramapithecus* we will find that he too is a man rather than an ape. I am going to suggest that neither of these was the real Adam, but in order to argue this point, I need first to draw attention to an unexamined assumption which tends to distort this kind of inquiry.

As concerns the first appearance of man, we tend unconsciously to think in terms of the biblical tradition of an instantaneous creation. We tend to assume, even when we think in evolutionary terms, that one day (or in one millennium or one epoch), man more or less suddenly appeared. Yet it is clear that the appearance of man was a gradual event stretched over a very long period of time measured in millions of years. Because the evolutionary process is so drawn out, it is impossible to say when one species of animal has given place to another. Speaking in terms of grades tends to obscure this fact, since grades constitute artificial, more or less arbitrary breaks in what in fact was an endless sequence of successive generations, each very much like its predecessor. Even with grades, however, it can be difficult to say when advanced apes have been replaced by primitive men.

*Ramapithecus* and *Australopithecus* are termed hominids because they had some of the characteristics of modern man, and in particular because they had upright posture and the ability to use tools. I do not object to calling them hominids on those grounds. Let us say they were hominids. But then to be a hominid need mean no more than that you are a bipedal, tool-using primate. It describes you and me. But it also describes Pliocene and Pleistocene primates whose small brains and primordial cultures make them seem far more akin to progressive apes than to *Homo sapiens*.

Call these earlier creatures hominids if you will, but let it be clearly understood that man as we know him today did not appear until much later. Who was Adam? If Adam was capable of family loyalty, if Adam had a soul, if he could speak, then Adam was *Homo erectus* and lived at least 300,000 years ago. But if in addition to these gifts, Adam had a sensitivity which made him care tenderly for his less fortunate kinsmen and worry about their souls when they died, then Adam was Neanderthal man of roughly 125,000 years ago. Or, if Adam had all of these abilities, but surpassed them in the poetic synthesis made possible only by art, music, and dance, and if Adam had a brain shaped for the first time just like ours, then Adam was *Homo sapiens* of as early as perhaps 40,000 years ago. Finally, if Adam was the first man to evolve a way of life that survived into historic and modern times as hunting and gathering peoples who laid the groundwork for the rise of civilization, then he was Mesolithic man of no more than some 20,000 years ago.

Who was Adam? He never existed. At no one point did the ape suddenly become a man. Over several million years, man's humanity grew. It is growing still, and our understanding of this gradual process in distorted if we attempt to interpret it in terms of prescientific concepts.

The Middle Pleistocene was a time of warm weather, since most of it coincided with the exceedingly long Second Interglacial period. Humanity took a giant stride forward as men of the grade *erectus* evolved organically and culturally in ways vastly different from what *Australopithecus* had been before. Human characteristics which still linger in us first emerged at that time.[1]

*Erectus* was completely modern in postcranial anatomy. His stature fell within the shorter end of the range for modern nonpygmy man. Cranially, he was still primitive. Java man, one of the earlier of the species, had a cranial capacity of approximately 875 c.c., well below the normal range of living men, and only slightly higher than that of gorillas. As the Second Interglacial progressed, the *erectus* brain evolved until in Peking man it came to vary around the 1,100 c.c. mark. Since most modern men range between 1,350 and 1,550 c.c., 1,100 represents notable progress in the human direction. The shape of the *erectus* brain is significant, however. Even in Peking man, it was relatively large in the back, but low in the vault and distinctively constricted in the frontal area. That most human part of the brain, the cerebral cortex, was not yet fully developed in this species.

Technologically, *erectus* remained relatively undeveloped for a very long time. The simple stone tools made by *Australopithecus* were scarcely improved upon. In the East, such tools, though better made, persisted throughout the Lower Paleolithic as the characteristic technological solution to human survival needs. In Africa, however, a new tradition emerged. Considerably more elaborate than the old Oldowan tool, the rough Abbevillian hand ax appeared, made by chipping away over most of the surface of the implement to give a cutting edge along two sides, drawing to a point at the end. With time, a smoother, slimmer, and better-cutting version appeared, the Acheulian. Its refined shape suggests that it was hafted somehow and wielded with speed and force. It looks like man's first effective hunting weapon.

These bifacially worked tools not only cut better than older chopping tools, they yielded roughly shaped chips in their manufacture which themselves were useful as scrapers and cutters, particularly for the kind of big game which probably was gotten with Acheulian techniques. In England, some of these Lower Paleolithic hunting and gathering peoples learned to depend much more on the flakes than on hand axes, anticipating in their so-called Clactonian industry the later abandonment of heavy bifacial tools for lighter, sharper, flake implements.

Man's capacity to manipulate his environment broadened as he added the hunting of larger animals to older techniques of foraging for vegetable food and small game. By the end of the Lower Paleolithic, when Abbevillian-Acheulian industries were known beyond Africa throughout the Western World as far east as India and as far north as Europe, human dexterity and cultural achievement had progressed to associate with hand axes the manufacture of well-shaped flake knives identified in the literature as Levalloisian.

No longer simply the more or less accidental by-products of ax production, Levalloisian flakes required very careful manipulation to produce. Selecting a large piece of suitable material, the stoneworker (knapper) struck away at it, probably with a straight piece of antler or hard wood, but perhaps simply by hitting it against an anvil stone, shaping it into something resembling the shell of a tortoise. Then, carefully notching out the precise place for a critical blow (preparing the striking platform), he hit the stone against an anvil to knock off a chip which, in effect, was pre-shaped to constitute a scraper or cutter with a clean, even edge and a thin body. The core could then be quickly reshaped to strike off a second flake, so that very rapidly, once the initial preparation was completed, a whole collection of well-formed tools could be produced. With the Levalloisian technique, man's dexterity reached a new level of achievement, and his capacity to live by hunting as well as by gathering was enhanced.

The appearance of better tools, particularly the Acheulian and Levalloisian, apparently reflects a greater development of the brain than was characteristic of earlier men. The cerebellum, with large parts involved in control of the thumb and hand, is three times as large in modern man as in the great ape. Undoubtedly, this part of the brain had to develop before refined tools could be made. The larger brains of Peking man and other late forms of *Homo erectus* apparently reflect this greater size of the cerebellum. Handedness may also have appeared at this time, since it is more efficient, both physiologically and psychologically, to concentrate training for dexterity in one hand or the other.

Sherwood L. Washburn and his students have pioneered in developing our thinking on these matters through their work on the behavior of living subhuman primates, particularly as they relate primatological observations to the archeological evidence for early man, on the one hand, and to the ethnographic evidence for recent and contemporary hunting and gathering peoples on the other.[2]

Their thinking goes something like this,[3] and it is admittedly very speculative. Like other animals that hunt, when man became a predator he had to extend his range in order to find enough game to live on. Nonhuman primates spend their whole lives within extremely limited territories. Most never move beyond a two- or three-square-mile area, and even the gorilla and baboon stay within approximately fifteen square miles. Modern human hunters, in contrast, range over territories of from 250 to 600 square miles. This shift to hunting over a large territory had implications for human culture. Presumably a new kind of cooperation appeared within the local group. Among lower primates, once weaned, each individual feeds himself. A mother and baby baboon, for example, may enjoy a close relationship, but as they grub for the sweet roots of savannah grass, the baby feeds itself and the mother herself, totally without the exchange of food.

Man the hunter relies upon a division of labor in order to procure an adequate diet. While the male ranges after game, away perhaps for several days at a stretch, the female cares for children and searches locally for wild fruit, vegetables, nuts, insects, birds, and other food. It is possible that women typically produced much more food than men. Yet, in the rounded diet, each produced a component which then was combined with others to feed everyone.

The family probably emerged in its present basic form at this time. Lower primates have familylike alliances, but in most cases the only enduring tie appears to be between mother and offspring. With a division of labor, the father became an integral part of this primordial unit. The new family arrangement appears related to biological changes in man. A more stable kind of family probably was needed because the period of dependence in immature offspring grew much longer. In part, the longer postpartum period of immaturity seems related to larger brain size. More time was needed for the cranium to grow to adult dimensions; the birth canal could pass the head of a baby only at an early stage in its growth. But in addition, the time required to learn how to cope culturally with staying alive also increased. There was so much more to learn than there once had been.

The new family seems associated with changes in the reproductive cycle. Female monkeys and apes experience an estrous cycle, in which sexual activity is limited to a rutting season. Human females undergo a menstrual cycle which allows them to be continuously receptive throughout the year. At some time, and for reasons we can only guess at, the estrous cycle became menstrual in the human line. Perhaps this change took place when the nature of the family changed. A sexually receptive woman would have given her man something additional to come home to. If that is so, then biological as well as cultural changes can be assumed to have taken place as correlates of a new, uniquely human kind of family.

Band organization emerged. Large animals could not be hunted successfully with only hand axes as weapons. More useful even than tools, no doubt, were techniques of social organization which regulated mutual aid in running down, trapping, and dispatching large game. Men could gang up on an animal, and that was their most effective weapon. Perhaps *Australopithecus* moved in small groups. For *erectus* it would have been a necessity.

As part of this hominid revolution, kinship ties beyond the family probably evolved into a social network that joined band members to individuals in other areas. It seems likely that incest rules appeared at this time to play an important role in man's growing humanity. Nonhuman primates probably had mother-son sexual avoidance. The evidence is not conclusive, but from the study of Japanese macques, it appears that, among monkeys, special ties relate mother to son throughout their lives. In human society, however, incest extends beyond that to include father and daughter as well as brother and sister. Generally it extends even wider.

There seem to be various reasons for the appearance of human incest rules. One suggested long ago by Westermarck is that sexual competition within the family would work against solidarity in this key group and therefore came to be forbidden. It seems clear that if brothers and their fathers were allowed to compete for sexual rights to the women in their family, they would not function well as a mutual aid group.

More recently, Washburn and his associates have suggested that incest taboos also have to do with the requirements of hunting. Sexual maturity in the male precedes by several years his maturity as a successful hunter. If a boy could have offspring by his sisters, the children would be fathered by a youth too young to feed them. Similarly, if the man could have offspring by his daughters, he would be fathering more children than he could nourish. The argument is not completely convincing, since most food probably derived from foraging, which adolescents could do as well as women. But to the extent a band relied upon hunting, the logic of this assumption holds.

Incest taboos constitute a precondition for local exogamy, the rule that marriage may take place only with someone from beyond the group. Primitive hunting societies have this rule as concerns the band, and Washburn has argued that it reflects covertly the need of small groups to be part of a large enough population to assure an approximately equal number of youths and maidens for marriage. Local exogamy, an extension of the concept of incest, is the foundation stone of ethnic identity, since it integrates each family into a wider network of people bound by the ties of intermarriage.

Religion too may have emerged as part of the changing quality of human life. From the remains of Peking man in the Choukoutien caves north of Peking we have a suggestion that ideas about supernatural phenomena had become part of the cultural inventory of early man. The nature of skeletal finds suggests cannibalism.[4] We think Peking man killed men he fought with, took their severed heads to his lair, and then bashed out the bottom of the skull to eat the brains. The fact that repeatedly we find no postcranial material, only the face and braincase with the bottom broken out, is the basis for this assumption. It is consistent with what we know of brain eaters elsewhere. It is also consistent with what we know ethnographically of cannibals to assume that eating the flesh of one's enemies was more a ritual than a gustatorial act.

In general, cannibals believe that by ingesting parts of the bodies of their enemies they somehow capture the enemy's power or control his soul. Since we infer that Peking man was a cannibal, it seems reasonable to infer further that he had at least the glimmerings of religious consciousness. A late *erectus* variety from Java, Solo man, also was a brain eater, further inclining us to see some religious belief and practice in at least the late phase of the Lower Paleolithic. Religion, then, may have appeared as part of a complex of traits having to do with band solidarity and the relationship of one band to another.

Finally and very importantly, true language probably appeared at this time.[5] For man to use tools of the sophistication of the Acheulian and Levalloisian types, words would have been useful as terms of reference. In order to hunt and fight in bands, he needed to be able to give and understand directions. Language serves this function well. In order to roam a large range and yet meet females and children at the home camp, he would have found it helpful to be able to make utterances concerning time and place. In order to develop concepts of incest and exogamy, he needed a terminology which incorporated these concepts and identified individuals as different kinds of kin or nonkin. In order to meet with friendly outsiders to arrange the exchanges of primitive marriage, he would have profited from language to create a community of discourse. And in order to develop and transmit ideas about the souls of men, he had to have names for intangibles.

Earlier grades may well have gotten along with no more than the emotional grunting and grimacing of nonhuman primates, expanded, probably, into some simple form of protolanguage. *Homo erectus* probably had true language as part of his cultural inventory. Correlated with this, part of his cranial anatomy no doubt included areas of the cerebral cortex associated with language and speech, specifically Brioca's Area, which is part of the supplementary motor cortex controlling speech; Wernicke's Area, which is that part of the auditory association area most involved with the sounds of words; and the Angular Gyrus, which serves a coordinating function.

The appearance of human language was so important that we must pause to examine its implications more closely. Years ago, Clarence Carpenter published a monograph in which he described how gibbons are capable of making nine different kinds of sound patterns, each apparently capable of communicating some simple idea.[6] In the early morning, for example, adult males make a series of hooting noises which apparently announce their location to others in the area and probably help groups to avoid conflict. When a strange creature appears to threaten them, any gibbon may give out a loud, high-pitched note or a shout to announce the alarm. Young animals when disturbed or confined in a cage cry in a kind of fretting way which has the appearance of being a begging gesture.

A number of psychologists have tried to teach chimpanzees to speak.[7] It is now clear that ape vocal cords, larynx, tongue, and lips are not capable of imitating human sounds. Under laboratory conditions, however, some psychologists in recent years have succeeded in teaching chimpanzees to use nonverbal language. David Premack, for example, trained a female named Sarah to communicate with human beings by using a "vocabulary" of about 130 plastic symbols that stand for things, actions, names, and even abstract ideas.[8] Besides remembering the shapes that stand for concrete objects such as "banana" or "apple," she recognizes those which symbolize verbs such as "take" and "give," as well as others which mean "good" and "bad." Sarah can organize her thoughts, it appears, and then arrange the metal-backed plastic chips on a magnetized board to express herself in simple sentences. She can respond to sentences written by her human friends.

In their natural habitat, however, apes do not use language. The best they can do is to communicate very simple meanings such as "food" or "danger." From an examination of the fossil record as well as what we know of ape communication, Charles Hockett and Robert Ascher have speculated that *Australopithecus* may have extended the call system of an ape into a kind of protolanguage.[9] By combining parts of different calls, precocious australopithecines may have introduced new sounds with new meanings. One can speculate, for example, that part of a sound for "food" could have been joined with part of a sound for "danger" to produce a new "word" meaning, roughly, "dangerous food, poison." Through such recombinations, an increasingly extensive vocabulary might have been built up. Over a long period of time, the first true language with associated developments of the brain may have occurred in this way.

Once true language had appeared, by whatever process, all populations would soon have learned to use it. "Any hominid groups that lagged behind in either the genetic or the cultural aspects of the transition from ape calls to human language would have suffered rapid extinction or confinement to narrow and undesirable habitats."[10] Because early language must have spread rapidly throughout the hominid world, and because early language is associated with related changes in the brain, it seems reasonable to assume that men in our time still share certain features of thought and speech. Many linguists lend support to this contention. Though still subject to debate, it appears that the enormous diversity of known languages overlays universals which make all men alike in fundamental ways of thinking (cognition).

We cannot yet completely identify and evaluate these universal qualities. Noam Chomsky and other linguists known as transformationalists recognize two levels of language, one called surface structure and the other, deep structure.[11] The surface structure is speech as we speak and hear it. But basic to the spoken word is a psychological level, the deep structure, where unconscious selection of basic units of thought is manipulated. Operations in the deep structure must be transformed into the speech of the surface structure, and it is the rules for making these transformations which particularly have been investigated. It appears that the deep structure is fundamentally the same in all men. Further, there may also be a universal set of transformation rules which each language builds upon in its own way.[12]

It is not necessary to turn to transformational grammar to find scholars advocating the existence of linguistic universals. Joseph Greenberg has made comparable claims based upon statistical studies, and Mary Le Cron Foster has identified what appear to be the sounds, meanings, and grammatical features of early language as they still exist, imbedded in known tongues.[13] In the nineteenth century, the anthropologist Adolph Bastian argued that underlying the great variability of human behavior are universally shared ways of thinking which he characterized as the psychic unity of mankind. Recent linguistic research has given a new basis for advocating this old point of view.

Language is much a part of the very process of thinking, so the language one speaks appears at once to reflect and to structure the way one thinks about things and takes action. In the words of Edward Sapir, "Language and our thought-grooves are inextricably interwoven, are, in a sense, one and the same."[14] Benjamin Whorf was the first to investigate more thoroughly just how speech, thought, and action may be interrelated, so the concept has often been designated as the Sapir-Whorf hypothesis. One of the many illustrations is the following:

> In a wood distillation plant the metal stills were insulated with a composition prepared from limestone and called at the plant "spun limestone." . . . After a period of use, the fire below one of the stills spread to the "limestone," which to everyone's great surprise burned vigorously. . . . Behavior that tolerated fire close to the covering was induced by use of the name "limestone," which because it ends in "stone" implies noncombustibility.[15]

In short, language can intervene between things and the way we react to them.

In recent years, a great deal of research identified as ethnoscience or cognitive anthropology, as well as by various other terms, has been directed toward gaining new insights into cultural differences by attempting to describe things and events as individuals in other cultures see them (the so-called emic view) rather than describing them in terms of the anthropologist's cross-cultural categories (the etic view).[16] Such work confirms the Sapir-Whorf hypothesis insofar as languages are found to differ greatly in the ways in which they structure men's world view or reflect it. Such work, however, should not be allowed to obscure the existence of an underlying psychic unity of mankind. No matter how different one language is from another, the message of the one can always be translated into the same message in the other. That is an important fact. Languages differ greatly from one another, but in their deep structure, in the underlying process of thinking, thought processes are universal, and therefore, ultimately, it is always possible for men to understand one another. Languages reflect differences, but they also reflect similarities.[17]

The end of the Lower Paleolithic was a time of important hominid changes, and language is an indication of these events. Once under way, however, still other significant developments took place to further distinguish men from their infrahuman predecessors.

The Middle Pleistocene gave way to the Upper Pleistocene as the Second Interglacial fell before the cold onslaught of the Riss glacial advance. When the Third Interglacial brought warmth again, man had progressed to the grade neanderthalensis, a level of development which was to persist into the early phase of the Würm glaciation.[18]

Neanderthal man was anatomically far advanced over his *erectus* ancestors and is perhaps best regarded as no more than a race of modern man, *Homo sapiens neanderthalensis*. His head and face seem somewhat primitive compared to modern man, with heavy brow ridges, a low, sloping forehead and depressed cranial vault, large, heavy facial bones, and marked facial prognathism and receding chin. But if the evolution of his brain was not yet as advanced as that of living men, it could not have fallen much short of it. His cranial capacity ranged generally between 1,350 and 1,400 c.c., fully within the range of modern men. One specimen measured 1,610 c.c., which would be very large even today.

Culturally, too, he was more advanced than his predecessors, enough so that the Mousterian assemblage, generally associated with Neanderthal man, is distinguished from earlier and later Stone Age developments as the Middle Paleolithic. This assemblage is characterized by a more varied tool inventory, a collection of finely made flint tools involving advances over older production techniques. The prepared core technique of the Levalloisian was improved upon as a hammer was substituted for the anvil stone to produce smaller, more finely made flake tools. These flakes were more symmetrical, with finer cutting edges and sharper points. Their quality was enhanced by secondary retouching, the knapper using a piece of bone, wood, or horn to press off microscopic flakes as he created straight, clean lines. The heavy hand ax went out of use, and its lightweight replacement was supplemented with the spear.

In the Lower Paleolithic, sharpened sticks with points hardened by carbonizing in a fire were sometimes used, for the end of such a spear was found in a Clactonian site. There is some evidence for the use of wooden spears in the Mousterian as well, but in some areas flint points notched for hafting indicate a considerable refinement of spear making and greater reliance upon it. Although without question, Neanderthal man still needed tightly organized mutual aid to bring down large animals, he had improved tools for the kill as well as for skinning and butchering.

Probably Neanderthal man was the first one to wear clothes. No doubt *Homo erectus* used some of his scrapers to prepare skins which could be thrown over the shoulders in cold weather. But Neanderthal man must have relied extensively on such clothing, because he not only made scrapers which could have been used to prepare skins, but for the first time he took up permanent residence in tundralike areas where he had to protect himself carefully with clothing in order to survive. This, in fact, is why primitive man is commonly thought of as a caveman. Living out the glaciation in Europe, where the weather was arctic or subarctic in severity, he had to have more than the simple lean-to or brush hovel which probably sufficed for earlier men. Caves were often used, and hence the popular but erroneous notion that all early men were "cavemen."

Living in a cave is a tricky business. It is cold and damp in arctic circumstances. It may also be the home of a bear or another dangerous animal. To keep warm and to frighten off predators, it helps to build a fire just inside the entrance. Peking man appears to have added fire to his cultural inventory in the Lower Paleolithic, but it was Neanderthal man who first learned to rely heavily upon it. Dirty black traces of hearths have been found at the mouths of caves containing the remains of Middle Paleolithic men. With fire, man got not only protection and warmth, however. He also could cook his food. Since cooking meat greatly increases the body's capacity to convert it into energy, it seems reasonable to assume that progress from this time on was stimulated by the greater capacity man now had for activity. But though man had learned to take fuller advantage of fire in the Middle Paleolithic, he did not necessarily know how to make it. It is reported that the Andamanese Islanders when first visited knew only how to maintain fires they had gotten from natural sources. The same thing may have been true of Neanderthal man.

Man's religiosity appears to have increased. Whatever the concept of the soul that lay behind the cannibalism of late Lower Paleolithic man, with the Middle Paleolithic it probably grew more complex. We cannot know what myths and beliefs flourished as men contemplated the awesome mystery of life and death. We do know that men ceased merely to discard their own dead kinsmen. At La Ferrassie in the Dordogne region of France, two adults and two children were found buried in shallow trenches. The method of burial suggests concern for the afterlife. The head of the man was protected by stone slabs. The arms of the woman had been folded and her legs pressed against her body, probably bound with thong. Some contemporary men have done this to prevent the dead from returning to haunt. Did Neanderthal man have such beliefs?

Elsewhere, too, we find graves for the first time in the history of man. But though deceased members of one's tribe were buried with religious fervor, the dead of the enemy still might be eaten. At Krapina in Yugoslavia, we have found what appear to be the remains of a grisly feast in which the entrée consisted of about ten men. At Monte Circeo, in Italy, the brain of a man was probably eaten, since a skull has survived which seems to have been broken open for this purpose.

Human sensitivity developed. Out of a cave at Shanidar in the Zagros Mountains of northern Iraq comes what may be tentatively interpreted as a most touching example of man's growing capacity to love his own kind.[19] One of three skeletons recovered apparently died accidentally when part of the roof of the cave fell in. On examination it became evident that at the time of death the subject was a male of approximately 40 years of age. Further examination, however, revealed some startling anomalies. It appeared that the right arm and shoulder had not developed normally and that the arm was missing below the elbow. Further, the subject was arthritic. From indications of excessive tooth wear we get a picture of a badly crippled man getting along around the camp by gripping things with his teeth, his good left hand, and the upper part of his withered right arm. Such a man could have been kept alive for so many years only because the members of his band had a high sense of his personal worth. In life as in death, the individual had gained a new identity; he had gotten a soul.

The early Würm glaciation stretched over northernmost Europe and then retreated. By the time of the main advance, Neanderthals had passed from the scene and fully modern man was present.[20] Just how the one grade led to the next is still not entirely clear. Most of what we know of the Middle and Upper Paleolithic is based upon finds made in the far west of the Old World, giving our interpretations a regrettable Eurocentric bias. Something of the process of change from Neanderthal to *sapiens* can be seen, however, in Mt. Carmel man. In a place known as the Cave of the Kids (Mugharet-es-Skhūl), a kind of transitional individual was found, what some authors have referred to as a sapienized Neanderthal. He had the cranial characteristics of a contemporary combined with very pronounced Neanderthaloid eyebrow ridges and facial projection (prognathism). With his skull in your hands, it really is not difficult to visualize both his Neanderthal ancestors and his fully *sapiens* descendants. The evolution of *Homo sapiens sapiens* out of *H. s. neanderthalensis* was no doubt a slow, very complicated process. We want to learn much more about it. But the change was sharp and dramatic in one sense. Neanderthals became extinct as a distinctive type of man.

The manual dexterity of early *sapiens* continued to improve, and his tool kit grew increasingly sophisticated.[21] Longer blade tools replaced the shorter flakes which had been used, and for this purpose a further modification of the prepared core technique was devised. In order to get long narrow flakes, the Mousterian disk core was replaced by one that was cylindrical. In order to concentrate the force of the blow precisely, blades were detached by using a punch instead of a hammer alone. Improvements in retouching techniques followed along, so that new tool shapes became possible. One such tool was a kind of knife blade manufactured with a blunt back so that it could be pressed down with the thumb when used to cut. No longer confined to tools with straight or broadly curving lines, insets could be made in the brittle flint to form specialized scrapers for grooving and burins for incising or drilling.

Among some Upper Paleolithic peoples, the use of bone expanded. Earlier men did not use much bone. Perhaps it was easier to shape wood, and in the East, bamboo may have been used, which would not have left records for the archeologist. But now we find bone much worked, shaped by the finer stone implements which were tools to make tools. And with the use of bone, new cultural achievements occurred. The presence of bone needles and awls suggests for the first time a refinement in clothing. Skins merely thrown over the shoulders or wrapped around the body were superseded, it appears, by tailored garments, far superior for living in cold climates, and still in use in the Arctic. Bone gorges looking something like tooth-picks pointed at both ends and waisted in the middle are good evidence for line fishing as an additional source of food. If not as convenient as the fishhook, the gorge still would have made man an effective fisherman in streams not yet fished out by large populations. Harpoon heads have also been recovered in considerable numbers, their shape unmistakable witness to a great refinement over the spear for hunting sea mammals and large fish.

In man's never-ending efforts to escape the limitations of his own body, two Upper Paleolithic developments are impressive. For the first time, man took advantage of basic physical principles to increase his mechanical advantage in throwing a spear. He invented the spear thrower. This is a piece of wood about as long as the forearm. One end is held in the hand. The butt of the spear fits into a notch at the other end. The effect is to add a new segment to the thrower's arm. It takes great skill to use, but is very effective in increasing the power and length of flight of a weapon. Also in the Upper Paleolithic, a few societies learned to use the bow and arrow. A very complex instrument, it too involves a principle of physics not formerly exploited. In drawing back his arrow, the bowman stores energy which can be released with sudden and deadly effect. With skill and experience, it too is a highly effective device.

The sophistication of religious practices also increased. In part this is revealed in burial customs. The relatively simple burials of the Neanderthals became elaborate in the Upper Paleolithic. It became customary to leave grave goods, objects of beauty and utility which the deceased might presumably use in his afterlife, symbols as well, no doubt, of the status and esteem enjoyed by the dead person. In some cases, the body was colored with red ochre. We find traces of it still on the bones after the fleshy parts have long since disappeared. Contemporary peoples who smear corpses with red ochre have the notion it ritually brings life again, the redness a simulation of living blood. Perhaps in the Upper Paleolithic men had similar beliefs about the afterlife and the need for the living to provide equipment and ritual rebirth for the dead.

We know more than this about Upper Paleolithic life, though, because as religion increasingly found expression symbolically in artifacts and social practices, it became associated with a wholly new component of the human potentiality, the first appearance of art. Art was a late but superlative achievement of the Stone Age.[22] Perhaps we glimpse a primitive artistic sensitivity in the finer shape of Mousterian tools or even in the refinements of the Acheulian hand ax. But at best, art through the Lower and Middle Paleolithic was no more than a primitive yearning. The higher mental endowment of Upper Paleolithic man, his greater dexterity, and his ability to control more than ever before both his environment and his own body were associated with the first achievements in art, music, and dance.

Almost all that we know concerns only the visual arts. In some Aurignacian assemblages, an early Upper Paleolithic tradition in Europe, we
find evidence of art production. It now appears, however, that Aurignacians
were influenced by immigrants from the East, and that the first real artists
in Europe were the so-called Gravettians.[23] Much of Gravettian art was in
the form of jewelry, men apparently as much addicted to its use as women.
The variety of this first known jewelry is impressive. It includes objects of
fired clay worn as pendants, beads of polished ivory, snail shells, mollusk
(dentalium) shells, fish vertebrae, and disks of mother-of-pearl. Most
beads were strung as necklaces, but some were apparently attached to hair
nets or clothing. Ivory plaque bracelets incised with geometric designs and
decorated pins combining utility and beauty were also made.

As men experimented with making things for the visual pleasure they
gave, one wonders if they were not impressed with the grandeur of their
own achievement. In billions of years, no creature before had ever done
such a thing. It inspired awe, no doubt, and it is therefore not surprising
that art early was associated with religion, with the supernatural. In the
plastic arts, this seems apparent in Gravettian-Aurignacian Venus figurines.
In a number of sites throughout the Upper Paleolithic we find small images
of women, notably distorted to exaggerate their female sexuality. Heads and
feet may be mere knobs, but breasts, buttocks, and thighs are dispropor-
tionately large. So frequently do they occur, and so vivid is their sexual
symbolism, that it seems fair to interpret them as the surviving visible remains of fertility cults, beliefs about an earth goddess who was the source
of life.

Aurignacians and Gravettians were also the first painters, and there too
we catch glimpses of developing religiosity. The earliest Aurignacian painting was rather undistinguished, except that painting was a wholly new
thing on the face of the earth. On the walls of rock shelters and caves,
artists drew or incised outlines of animals, particularly the foreparts. Undoubtedly they had a religious intent, but this is clearer where artists out-
lined crudely what appear to be the vulvas of females, for they may well
have been meant to symbolize in yet another way ideas about a fertility goddess.

Gravettians somewhat later did better in painting. They drew geometric
figures sometimes. They also showed human hands, apparently using their
own hands as stencils as they blew powdered paint onto the wet surface
of the wall. Again, religious concepts may have been present. Often the
hand seems to show part of a finger missing or several fingers. Among a
number of living peoples, an individual in deep mourning or anguish may
chop off the joint of a finger to placate the gods, and older individuals may
have several fingers missing as a result of such devotion. Perhaps the
custom was known to these Europeans of the Upper Paleolithic.

If the earliest Aurignacian cave art was done as long ago as 25,000 B.C., an approximate date, then the latest and best was done during the Magdalenian period, roughly between 15,000 and 8,300 B.C. In the passage of some 10,000 years, line drawings had become multicolored paintings that captured the drama and beauty of the animal world even though the artists never developed a three-dimensional perspective. With this perfection of skill, Upper Paleolithic man increased his commitment to religious activities. He still seemed concerned with fertility rites. Sometimes he showed animals copulating. But it seems likely he also had the notion that in painting an animal he somehow made that animal materialize in the hunt, and the many pictures of wild boar, deer, bison, and other animals possibly represented animals he hoped would be killed. More explicitly, in some instances these animals were painted with arrows or spears in their bodies, magically shot down, we may assume, in the dark interior of a cave, for these paintings are often found in hidden recesses where their beauty could be appreciated only by their creator, sacred altars as it were for the rite of the hunt.

Without doubt, every able-bodied man had to do his share of hunting in the Upper Paleolithic. Yet the great skill of Magdalenian painters suggests certain men specialized as sorcerers (shamans), doing their duty as magicians in hours when they were not on the trail. A few of their paintings give further hints. In some cases, men are portrayed disguised in animal skins, stalkers, perhaps, of unwary victims, but just as likely, medicine men whose dance to some kind of rhythmic beat was part of increasingly complex rituals of hunting magic.

The notion that music and dance were known is scarcely more than an educated guess. From what we know of living shamans whose dress and paraphernalia resemble those portrayed in the Magdalenian, it seems reasonable to assume some kind of simple music. Further, we have discovered the remains of what may have been a very ancient boys' initiation rite.[24] In a cave in southern France, far in the back, two-foot-high sculptures of bison were set up, one a cow being mounted by a bull. Around these bison, undisturbed for thousands and thousands of years, still can be seen the heel marks of juveniles. Because they are heels only, they may have been left from a kind of circular dance. And because they were made by youngsters, it seems reasonable that they were boys being initiated in the fertility rites that had already endured for millennia.

Inferences, inferences; we can only speculate. Upper Paleolithic man could produce art. He surely was religious, and it seems likely that the soul of the individual after death, fertility, and the hunt were focal aspects of his sacred life. Music, at least as basic rhythm, and dancing as part of ritual probably were present, but the conclusion remains vague and tenuous. Initiation rites for boys? Possible, certainly, but also a vague and tenuous assumption. Man's own view of himself and of his place in the cosmos had undoubtedly become a wondrous thing during the last glaciation, but we have more questions than answers as we probe these earliest indications of man's spiritual development.

As the last glaciation ebbed away and the warmer climate of our own time spread over the northern part of the world, and as in the south a warmer, drier climate appeared, the Upper Paleolithic gave way imperceptibly to the Mesolithic. Technologically, we have identified it as a period when man's control of nature took on new dimensions[25] Man learned to make composite tools by chipping off very small but extremely sharp flakes which, because they were about the size of a fingernail, could only be useful if set in rows in bone or wood. In this way, knives, saws, and spear points were manufactured. Line fishing improved as bone fishhooks were devised, and net fishing was employed, since we have found traces of nets and bark floats. The leister was developed for spearing fish; the harpoon continued to be used for larger sea mammals, but for fish, the three-pronged leister is much superior to either harpoon or spear. Shellfish began to be exploited as a major source of food, although some mollusks were collected in the Upper Paleolithic. But by this time, some settlements so depended upon crustaceans that over the generations their settlements grew into high mounds of discarded shells and other debris.

It is more than accidental that Mesolithic men learned to exploit the food resources of rivers, lakes, and seas. For the first time he probably mastered boating and, perhaps, swimming. We still have no remains of boats that old. But such heavy reliance upon fish and mollusks is itself suggestive of a new command over water. Boating not only would have opened up new food resources, it would have broken down barriers to travel as well. Whereas rivers, lakes, and open water previously had been blocks to easy movement, now they were highways, for it is quicker to travel by canoe than to go by foot.

On land, Mesolithic man's hunting capacity continued to improve. Bows and arrows, uncommon in the Upper Paleolithic, now became widespread. Dogs were domesticated and undoubtedly made men far better hunters than they had been, since they can be used for locating, tracking, cornering, and even killing game. Richard B. Lee reports that in a Bushman camp in which one hunter had a pack of dogs and six others did not, the man with the dogs brought in 75 percent of the band's meat, while the other six all together accounted for only the remaining 25 percent.[26]

The collecting of plant foods also improved. The first grinding stones came into use, suggesting that seeds were consumed. Seeds are valuable because they are among the few food items most hunting peoples can acquire which will not spoil, and they thus give some protection against winter starvation. Ground and boiled seeds may have been an important addition to the hunting economy of about this time.

Sherwood Washburn insists on the importance of cultural changes which took place in the Upper Paleolithic and the Mesolithic some 10,000 or 15,000 years before the first appearance of agriculture. "In the last few thousand years before agriculture," he writes, "both hunting and gathering became much more complex. This final adaptation, including the use of products of river and sea and the grinding and cooking of otherwise inedible seeds and nuts, was worldwide, laid the basis for the discovery of agriculture, and was much more effective and diversified than the previously existing hunting and gathering adaptations."[27]

Gradually, the gap between man and animal had grown to a giant chasm. Yet the Mesolithic was not so very long ago in the perspective we have adopted here, a mere 10,000 to 20,000 years or so. Some of those bands developed into more complex societies with elaborate technologies and other innovations. But some persisted from one millennium to the next without change in their basic style of life. Some of those surviving hunting bands endured into recent times, to be observed by trained ethnographers. A few still survive today. So with the Mesolithic we arrive at a kind of society which is part of our own world of today and of recent centuries. The present has its first living interface with the past in the Mesolithic.

# 4

# The Mark of Cain

With dramatic effect, the biblical story of Cain and Abel draws attention to a fatal truth about human beings. From the beginning, man has been different from lower animals because he alone is capable of killing his own kind. Other animals may be killers, and they may fight among themselves, but normally they stop short of dealing the death blow to individuals in their own group or to members of their own species. Yet Cain rose up against his brother Abel and killed him. As a consequence of this primordial murder, "the Lord put a mark upon Cain." And what was that mark? Biblical scholars have debated the question for centuries without reaching agreement, but this much is clear: Whatever else it may symbolize, the mark of Cain stands for a man who could kill his own brother. We all bear the mark of Cain in that sense.

Early man distinguished himself from still earlier, essentially vegetarian, browsing apes by becoming a hunter. Later, by improving his ability to hunt, he enlarged the difference between himself and all other living creatures. His humanity appears to have grown with perfectability of the capacity to kill. But skill in killing is volatile and dangerous. Directed against game, it ends in nourishment. But directed against other men, it brutalizes and destroys. The history of man, as a consequence, has been a history of controlling and directing, but sometimes also of succumbing to, the human propensity for aggression.

During the late Upper Paleolithic and Mesolithic periods an expanding human population pushed northward in the backwash of a receding Ice Age. In Siberia their pushing took them eastward and unknowingly onto a new continent. The Bering Straits at that time formed a land bridge over which men and dogs could easily make their way. Even later, when only islands remained, no stretch of open water was too great for primitive boats to traverse. Both hemispheres for the first time became occupied by men.

These early hunters had to cope with the dangers of aggression. How can we know how they did it? The archeological record, rich in physical remains, says nothing directly of human emotions or of social relations. Yet much social and psychological information about early hunters can be gained through the study of some living peoples. A few hunting and gathering societies survive to the present—Eskimo in arctic North America, Algonkian and Athapaskan caribou hunters in Canada, the Shoshone of the Great Basin in the American West, the Ona and Yahgan Indians of Tierra del Fuego at the southernmost tip of South America, the forest-dwelling pygmies of the African Congo, the Bushmen of South Africa, the aborigines of Australia, the pygmy Semang of the Malaysian rainforest, and the Andaman Islanders in the Bay of Bengal. From recent and contemporary societies, properly evaluated, we can draw inferences about the human condition at the hunting and gathering stage of existence. What we find is reassuring, for it suggests that man can live in relative peace, at least under some circumstances.

Let us take aggression to be "behavior where the goal is the injury of some person or object."[1] Many aspects of the human condition clearly are implicated in the working out of aggression. Because personality is involved, psychological factors are important. Insofar as ideas play a part, ideology is a consideration. Economics and technology are significant too. Some theorists today would stress underlying instincts as fundamental. Each of these aspects of human behavior might provide a gateway to the analysis of this complex topic, and one is not necessarily better than the other as a beginning. The gateway I have chosen, however, is none of these, though it incorporates elements of all. I choose to look at aggression in terms of the social structure, in terms, that is, of how one solves the dilemma of who may be attacked and who may not.

Man the hunter lived in small, scattered families and bands. In order to nourish themselves by foraging and hunting, populations had to be thin, a scattering of small encampments. Food was not plentiful enough to support large groups. Nor could the population be entirely sedentary under ordinary circumstances. Hunters generally had to move from one part of their territory to another on a regular seasonal basis in order to take advantage of wild seeds, nuts, fruits, and vegetables as they matured, or fish and game as they became plentiful. The hunting and gathering technology traditionally did not include effective ways to preserve food, although there are some exceptions. So ecological forces were at work to limit effectively most peoples to small groups of seminomads.

To some extent the hunter had to face a fickle world with only his family to rely upon. With his wife or wives and children, he might at times go off on his own. Most commonly, though, the smallest viable grouping was a number of these domestic families, a band. Grouping families together had important advantages in addition to the pleasure of company. Women could help one another with the care of infants and small children. Men could work together to hunt, sometimes better able that way to encircle the prey, but above all able to maintain a kind of meat bank for participating families. The hunt, after all, is an uncertain occupation. Today's success can be followed by failure for days. When a group includes several men out hunting, the chances are that one will succeed even if others do not. By sharing throughout the band whatever meat is gotten, and hunting societies everywhere have had firm rules for sharing game, every family can have some meat even when success is meager.

The way people grouped into bands was culturally patterned.[2] Fundamental everywhere was a band made up of a core of kinsmen living on a more or less circumscribed territory. Typically, the heart of the band comprised half a dozen to twenty or more adult men related as brothers, fathers, and sons; they were bound by the ties of patrilineage. Men related in other ways might be attached to the group, but the core was a cluster of close kinsmen. Elman R. Service finds the key to this kind of band organization in two rules of marriage. One is the custom of band exogamy, which simply means that it was forbidden to marry someone you have grown up with. You had to find your spouse in another band. The other is the rule that it was the woman who went to live with her husband after marriage (patrilocality), not the other way around.

The band which resulted from these two rules of kinship and marriage is termed patrilocal by Service. By this term, he draws attention to the territorial solidarity of a group formed by older men with their sons and sons' wives and attached to a hunting and foraging range by the custom of living with the groom's parents after marriage.

In some parts of the world, the ties of kinship which unite families into bands are amorphous. It does not seem to matter whether the tie is through males or through females, so long as a tie exists. Professor Service terms such societies composite bands, and speculates they once were patrilocal, but have changed as a result of contact with more advanced peoples. Aboriginal bands break up under pressures of warfare, expropriation of territory, dissipation of game reserves, and ravages of unaccustomed diseases. Old rules of marriage and alliance give way to the *ad hoc* arrangements which, as Service has put it, have more in common with refugee camps than with primeval bands. Even so, the band still tends to unite as a group of related families in which the etiquette of kinship is fundamental to social order.

What can you do if a member of your band becomes aggressive? How do you cope with a brute or a murderer? You cannot rely upon formal authorities, for none exists. Those who appear to be leaders have almost no real power. One man may quietly take the lead as the most capable hunter. Another may direct a complex ceremony by virtue of his age and experience. In no case will such men normally give direct orders, however, for the ethos is egalitarian and the mode of decision making is consensus.

And no leader formally holds the position of judge or sheriff. When an individual in the camp becomes a threat, the adult men may be expected to discuss the problem and to search for a solution, but their alternatives will not include referral to formal authority. Rather, they may be expected to work within the framework of the kinship system.

Kin loyalties are the strongest human bonds for hunters, forming a network of reciprocal rights and obligations sanctioned by a sense of sacred duty. An individual who becomes aggressive within the band threatens this sacred network, and while an occasional harsh act, a certain amount of friction, may go unchecked, a large or persistent threat will be countered, informally but effectively, as kinsmen conclude among themselves how to do it. A murderer, to take the most serious of offenders, will find no refuge as he flees, for other bands will generally accept only kinsmen, and even related bands will sooner or later learn that the newcomer is dangerous. Within his own band, the murderer must expect fatal retribution. His own brother or cousin will execute a punishment agreed upon within the band— he will be killed.

If the offender is not a murderer, other effective ways of dealing with him may be used. Another member of the band may challenge him. The duel, though, is normally diverted from reliance upon brute force to some form of ritualized ordeal. Among Australian aborigines, for example, the dispute may be settled by a fight with throwing spears, the loser suffering a flesh wound as his punishment. Among the Eskimo of Greenland, a wrestling contest or a song duel may be initiated. Song duels require each man alternately to attack the other with a kind of musical rhetoric, insults and diatribes winging back and forth to attack the good name of each. The loser suffers shame rather than physical hurt, a serious punishment in any small society. Interestingly, the winner of a duel is not necessarily the best improviser of songs, the best wrestler, or the best man with a spear. In any kind of band-level contest, the decisive element is audience reaction as onlookers praise or ridicule the contestants. The contestant in Australia who has lost the support of the crowd simply gives up and accepts his wound, however painful to pride and body. Similarly, the crowd judges the Eskimo in his duels, and the wrestler or singer loses the fight who loses rapport with observers. In this public forum, the offender is chastised, justice is done, aggression is curtailed.

Aggression between bands generally is siphoned off in comparable ways. The only technique for fighting is feuding. One man with his kinsmen may carry on a kind of guerrilla warfare with his enemy and his kin. The feud, though, is a costly way to battle, primarily because it has no mechanism for efficient termination. Once well under way, it tends to go on indefinitely as one side or the other feels it still has its due to extract. Feuds begin from time to time, but hostility is typically short-lived as someone intervenes to work out a settlement.

Commonly, the mediator of a dispute is a kinsman to both men, preferably equally related to each, so that his impartiality will not be suspect. The aggressor will be forced, because his own family is important to him, to give in, to indemnify, to desist from future hostility. If his aggression requires the expiation of punishment, even death, he will get it at the hands of his own close relatives, for the security and reputation of the band as a whole is more important than the happiness or life of a brother who is immoral. So effective are these attitudes and techniques that fighting between bands is as rare as brutality within a band. "Peace within the band is the normal condition," writes Elman Service. "It is also rare," he goes on, "that there is actual fighting among bands."[3] Man's capacity for aggression remains directed against the wild animals which are his prey.

The hunter became a tiller or a herder. Customarily, we speak of this change as the advent of the Neolithic or New Stone Age. The archeologist sees it in his excavating as a new level of technological development.[4] He uncovers stone axes or adzes much more efficient for heavy chopping because they are made of harder stone shaped by new techiques of grinding, chipping, and polishing. With ground stone tools, fields could be cleared of trees and brush so that crops could be sown, for the dominant feature of the Neolithic is the development of food production, the first appearance of cultivators. Ceramic pots made their appearance as storage containers for grain, and substantial houses for the first time became common.

Houses, fields, and pots are indicative of a new mode of life. Men settled down. Even though they continued to hunt, fish, and forage, as they became increasingly dependent upon their own fields they found it expedient to build more substantial villages and hamlets where year-round residence became the norm. With grain stored in pots and baskets, men could better survive the extremes of feast and famine. Being settled in one place, they no longer had to limit their material possessions to what could be carried on their backs or stored in hidden caches. Wealth began to accumulate. Pots and baskets and tools and fine clothes could be collected. And pervading all of these interests and activities was further development of religious beliefs and practices.

Under the new regime, priests or shamans could find the time to undertake sacred duties. They perfected their arts. Much wealth and time apparently went into elaborating vital activities. Fertility rites developed as communal acts to ensure success at planting time, to bring rain when needed, and to give thanks for the harvest when it came. Initiation rites and curing ceremonies as well as the celebrations of births and deaths continued as sacred preoccupations. On the material side, works of art became richer and more splendid as supplements to religious activities. Sculptured representations of spirits and gods, carved fetishes, elaborate masks, costumes, and other decorative objects were created to complement a growing complexity in music, dance, and oral poetry and legend.

Pastoralists, a different kind of food producer, also appeared during the Neolithic. Cattle breeders on foot typically maintained permanent settlements as substantial as those of horticulturalists, though their villages might be virtually abandoned at seasons when the herds must be away. They too could accumulate wealth and invest in ceremony. Even pastoralists who rode, whether on horses, camels, or reindeer, though living in tents, could acquire great wealth, for unlike the simple hunter, it was possible for them to pack and carry large amounts of goods.

These Neolithic circumstances also characterized some relatively rare non-food producers of about the same time as well as a millennium or so earlier. Where natural resources were unusually rich, village life could appear. Great salmon runs off the North Pacific, for example, provided an economic base for village life. So did acorns in aboriginal California and shellfish in a number of coastal areas. Although atypical of people with a Mesolithic technology, a few did anticipate major elements of the Neolithic achievement. On the whole, however, the level of cultural development we are discussing is associated with food production and got its start around 8,000 to 10,000 years ago in the Old World and approximately 7,000 years ago in the New World, the two centers emerging independently in each place.

Once food production made its appearance, the new style of life spread at the expense of the old.[5] Wherever hunting and gathering territories were suitable for cultivation or grazing, they were converted. Much of this change apparently took place as a growing population searched for new land. More numerous and better organized than scattered bands of hunters, villagers could overwhelm them by force. Often, however, it seems the newcomers absorbed and assimilated older populations, bands disappearing as discrete societies but surviving as they gave an old coloration to new customs. No doubt many bands more or less spontaneously became extinct as encroaching farmers or herders left them demoralized. And many, too, beat the newcomers to the punch by copying their way of life and staying on as New Stone Age men.

Whatever their fate, hunting societies as such disappeared except in marginal areas, where deserts, dense forests, or arctic climates made horticulture and pastoralism unprofitable. Each millennium and even each century saw their numbers and territory shrink. By approximately 2000 B.C., most of the territory of Eurasia was inhabited by Neolithic peoples. The same was true in Africa and Oceania by around A.D. 1000, although South Africa and Australia were notable exceptions. Most of the aborigines of Australia remained at the band level of development until the nineteenth century. By the time of the Conquest, say, A.D. 1500, the Americas mostly were occupied by Neolithic societies or higher civilizations, although a large expanse in the northern part of North America and smaller hinterland areas, including Patagonia and Tierra del Fuego, remained in the hands of hunters and gatherers. By the late nineteenth and early twentieth centuries, out of a world once solely populated by hunting and foraging societies, only a few still existed.[6]

The habitable earth was conquered by Neolithic (tribal) peoples. It was conquered as well by endemic warfare. Most New Stone Age men were fighters. It would be mistaken, however, to see a resurgence at this time of a long-dormant, animal-like instinct to hold and defend territory, as Robert Ardrey, Konrad Lorenz, or Desmond Morris have argued in the last few years.[7] It is abundantly clear that territory in itself cannot cause men to fight. As the foundation of all wealth, the land has always been basic to social relationships. But as a subject of discord, it has been an issue of warfare in some places but not in others. Men do not fight over territory as such, but over the uses that can be made of land and the things which can be produced on it, including people. Whether they fight over land, therefore, depends in part on how the land is used. This is true in our time. It has been true in the past. Who among us will not normally give up with pleasure, and certainly without a fight, whatever land he owns or uses in return for something as organically insignificant as a check made out for a large sum of money!

Dominance behavior, always a feature of Primate social life, seems more likely to lie behind human aggression. Men, apes, and monkeys still remain alike insofar as their group life may allow for or be influenced by certain individuals who dominate the rest. Dominance rather than the territorial imperative is an urge which affects all Primates, including man.[8]

Dominance, however, does not normally result in fighting. On the contrary, it can provide the basis for peace. As Irven De Vore and Sherwood Washburn found from their study of baboon troops, precisely because a few males are clearly in command, very little fighting normally takes place. Everyone knows his place. Only occasionally, and briefly, does fighting erupt when a change in rank order takes place. And in such fights, the loser is not normally killed, though his wounds are serious in some cases.[9]

Dominance may provide the emotional energy that men need to fight other men, but something has to trigger it off if it is to result in recurrent fighting. That something is culture. Men can and have lived together in peace. But when the norms men live by support and encourage warfare, they will fight. Such norms found a fertile breeding ground in the Neolithic. The new way of life seemed to nourish a warlike ideology.

In part, warfare apparently took root in the Neolithic because of new opportunities to accumulate wealth and to cultivate greed. In Africa, Nuer cattle herders raid more remote tribesmen or the neighboring Dinka for cattle. They may also lay claim to the territory of enemies, but only so they can maintain larger herds. They are robbers—no more and no less—and they are threatened by robbers.[10] Similarly as concerns the horticultural Yanomamö of the Brazilian-Venezuelan rainforest.[11] Raiding parties try to steal young women from weaker communities. When villagers are attacked, the men fight to save their lives and keep their women. The men in a raiding party have land enough around their own settlement; they do not normally need more. Each man, dependent on family labor, can cultivate only a certain amount. Nor, for that matter, do Yanomamö cultivators feel some inchoate need to defend their home territories as such. Weaker communities, in fact, frequently move to other areas where they are less threatened by powerful enemies. It is not the land which is important to them, but the people and wealth on it.

Population density as much as greed seems to have encouraged aggressiveness among early tribal peoples. Larger communities and more densely settled regions made their appearance at this time. With a higher population density, the minor frictions of social life appear to have more serious consequences. Among the Jivaro of eastern Equador, for example, a quarrel may start if one man's untended pigs wander into another man's unwatched fields and ruin his crops. Individuals may abuse each other if one man steals or seduces the wife of another. The many such frictions of a more intense social life can lead to quarreling. Later, when an individual falls ill or dies, one easily concludes that sickness or death have been magically sent in retaliation, and the quarrel escalates. Similarly with the Maori of New Zealand. Occasionally men raided to steal, but mostly they fought to redress real or imagined injuries suffered by villagers in contact with one another.

With greed and crowding more or less universal problems, most tribal people typically live in a world continually at a low boil of quarreling, feuding, and raiding.[12] In every tribe, the organization of society must, above all, modulate and govern aggression. But for the most part, failure is more common than success; forces for war generally are more powerful and better organized than forces for peace. Witness, for example, the Nuer.[13]

The Nuer fight for various reasons. Within a community and between villages, quarrels develop when one man's millet is eaten by another man's cow or goat, when one man strikes another man's son, when a dance ornament or other object is borrowed without permission, or when men disagree over water and pasture rights. Frequently it is the ownership of cattle which leads to trouble. The men of a village or a locality, even of a single homestead, will fight readily over a cow. More distant members of the tribe are still more inclined to dispute the ownership of animals or the division of stolen wealth. Between tribes of the Nuer or between the Nuer and the Dinka, thieving may take place with no more provocation than the greed of a raiding party which thinks itself strong enough to carry off its plan.

Within the household and the locality, the small-scale mechanisms of surviving band organization generally siphon off the hostility of disagreements to maintain the peace. Elders and kinsmen mediate. Feuds between neighboring villages rarely endure. More distant settlements in a tribe, however, are more likely to continue a feud and to escalate it. No one has authority to adjudicate and settle such a fight, though a Leopard-Skin Chief, a man religiously respected and considered neutral in mundane disputes, might be asked to mediate, and might be successful. But the more distant the ties between two men, the more likely a feud is to smolder on, and no mechanisms exist to arbitrate the hostility of one tribe for another.

Mechanisms for moderating and terminating feuds and fights grow increasingly ineffectual or are nonexistent as the distance between the disputants increases. But while the social structure is defective in institutions for peace, it is effective in institutions for war. Reliance upon a core of kinsmen, fundamental to cooperation in bands, is elaborated among the Nuer, as it typically is among tribal-level peoples, in a lineage and clan system.

Beyond one's immediate male relatives, a man maintains especially close ties to a patrilineal group which can be quite large because it may embrace the offspring of brothers who lived as much as five or six generations earlier. This is the lineage.

In some tribal groups, descent is traced matrilineally rather than otherwise. Matrilineal tribes usually are horticulturists, and it is perhaps because the more important tie is to land tilled by the women rather than to a group of men who hunted, fished, or herded that kinship is reckoned in the female line. But whether matrilineal or patrilineal, larger groups are important for tribes.

Beyond the lineage, ties in either the male or the female line, unilineal ties, identify a rather large number of people so distantly related that the exact links have been forgotten. Yet because a sense of kinship persists, such a group normally considers marriage within the group incestuous. This type of large, unilineal, exogamous entity is a clan, and is composed of a number of families and lineages able to claim common ancestry through either the male or the female line, but not both, from a distant, usually mythological, ancestor. And as in tribes generally, clans are important units of Nuer society. They vary in the extent to which they constitute territorial as well as kinship groupings, however. Among the Nuer, clans and lineages are only incompletely territorial.

Nuer villages as well as larger geographical segments of the tribe appear once to have been kinship entities. But cattle breeding is a hazardous occupation. The livelihood of a family can be destroyed overnight by a raid or epidemic. Famine or drought in one area may force families to migrate. With the passage of years, some localities have lost most of their founding families. Others have gained many refugees or immigrants. In these ways, though territorial groups are still regarded as kinship units, the dominant lineage may actually constitute a minority in its own geographical segment. Even so, the core population of a Nuer tribe is made up of the men of a dominant clan, just as a segment of the tribe corresponds roughly to a lineage of the dominant clan.

As far as personal loyalty is concerned, an individual belongs to a pyramid of bigger but increasingly remote groups. The smallest and most important unit is a man's hut, where he lives with his wife and children. The hut may be part of a homestead, where it clusters with the huts of other of his wives or of close kinsmen. But these domestic units are themselves elements of hamlets, and the hamlets, of villages. All who belong to these basic groupings normally are related at least as in-laws. Within the village, members work together in herding and other tasks and often eat at one another's hearths. The inhabitants of a village have been characterized by Evans-Pritchard as having a strong sense of solidarity vis-à-vis other villages. As long as a dispute is with someone from outside the village, a man can count on the other men of his community to stand by him in a fight. And here is where an important technique of organization is brought into play, one termed the segmentary principle.

According to the segmentary principle, fission and fusion in political organization take place with equal ease and rapidity. Fission is the normal state. Ordinarily, men live in terms of their families, hamlets and villages. But with warfare, villages fuse, whether in offense or defense. Just how many villages fuse for the fight depends upon the circumstances, but large war parties can be organized in this way. A fight may merely pit one village against another, but it may also oppose one half of the tribe against the other half, one Nuer tribe against another, or a Nuer tribe against the neighboring Dinka.

When the war is over, the structure collapses. Each man returns to his village and once again limits his cooperation to that level. In order to defend themselves or to attack, the Nuer can manage for the time being to throw aside lesser antagonisms to pursue a larger goal. The social structure works with reasonable effectiveness to organize for war, but not for peace. Therein lies the sociological foundation for endemic warfare among the Nuer.

The Plains Indians of North America provide an interesting contrast.[14] They too lived in a world endlessly simmering on the coals of attack and revenge. They too relied heavily on lineage and clan as organizational principles. Yet their political organization operated rather differently. They relied essentially on informal, though highly patterned, procedures for organizing warfare, and they utilized the formal social structure to work primarily for peace. Yet peace proved hard to maintain.

Every boy was brought up passionately to want to gain fame as a warrior. From babyhood he was taught to be tough and to endure pain. When big enough to fight, he hoped to capture scalps, since acquiring the soul power of his enemies enhanced his own strength. Through success in fighting his status grew. Plains tribes, in fact, had elaborate, highly artificial ways of recognizing success. Among the Blackfoot, for example, the most prestigious acts were capturing the weapon of an enemy, taking a scalp, or touching the adversary with one's hand or a special stick, an act known as counting coup. The Crow, by comparison, worked to earn credit in four stereotyped ways: leading a successful war party, counting coup, stealing a tethered horse, and capturing the weapon of an enemy in hand-to-hand combat.

Special privileges belonged to the successful warrior. In tribal gatherings, he had the honor of reciting his lifetime of exploits to the gathered host. On his robe or tepee, he was entitled to have paintings illustrating his major feats of derring-do. And on his costume he wore symbols of rank as obvious and well understood as the emblems of modern twentieth century soldiers. Assinboin and Dakota warriors wore eagle feathers as measures of their stature, the number of feathers corresponding to the number of praiseworthy deeds. Not all Plains Indians developed feather heraldry, however. The Blackfoot scarcely used feathers, preferring white weasel skins instead, and the Crow, depending upon the deed, wore wolf tails, ermine skins, or hair trimming on their shirts and moccasins.

Plainsmen, then, were brought up to find themselves individually as warriors. They fought to gain social standing among their people. Most raiding, though, had the more direct goal of stealing horses. Often a war party spent several days marching on foot to the attack, planning to ride captured horses on their return.

Whatever their direct motivation, organization of a raid depended upon personal or charismatic leadership. A warrior wanting to lead a war party simply made his plans known and recruited volunteers. If he had a record of success, if his "medicine" was powerful, he might get a rather large, strong group. A young man had to be satisfied with a few companions. Larger forces of 100 or 200 could be organized only by highly successful chiefs, and they were rare. Not until tribal defeat was already imminent at the hands of the American cavalry did Indians learn to fight as tribes and confederations of tribes. By then it was too late. They were overwhelmed by superior weaponry and organization. But always they had found it easy to organize small raiding parties against the camps of hostile tribes.

The challenge for the Plains Indian was not to organize warfare but to control it. Plains tribes had chiefs; generally, however, chiefly status implied prestige but not power. Leadership required consensus on the part of all warriors, the chief merely acting as spokesman for the council. Councils tended to be rather fluid institutions, variable with the composition of the group and the exigencies of the moment. Chiefs and councils frequently attempted to use their prestige and position to discourage rash young men whose need for glory could bring disaster to the encampment. "Any suggestion of taking up the war hatchet," Kaj Birket-Smith writes, "certainly could not originate with the chiefs: they were in duty bound to strive for the maintenance of peace."[15] In spite of their efforts, however, warriors continued to fight.

Clans were prominent in Indian organization. Yet they were important primarily for regulating marriage or for invoking broad moral obligations, and functioned only inchoately to organize for either war or peace.

No account of Plains Indian social organization would be complete without a place in it for formal voluntary associations. On the plains, men formed groups in which the tie binding them together was neither territory nor proximity, as in camps and villages, nor kinship, as in lineages and clans. Rather, the groups were formed on the basis of some common interest or shared concern. Such groups are very rare in band society, although occasionally they occur. Among Australian aborigines, for example, the members of each totem cult were bound together by a shared responsibility to a sacred totem, more or less independent of band and family ties as such. At the tribal level, associations are common. Often they are very important. Even among the Nuer they existed as age sets, the special ties uniting boys initiated in a common rite. On the plains, associations were highly elaborated as institutions additional to those of territory and kinship.

Long ago, A. L. Kroeber pointed out that for the Zuñi Indians of the Southwestern United States, if only territorial and kin ties were important, the society would tend to divide into opposing groups; it would fission.[16] But it did not, perhaps largely because common interest ties cut across the divisive ties of soil and blood. Associations recruited from different kinship groups. This principle applies as well among the Nuer and other tribal peoples. Among the Nuer, boys are initiated every few years in rites which take place simultaneously in communities throughout the tribe. The event is a time to give tribal marks to boys. Aged around fourteen to sixteen, the initiates lie on their backs as an elder cuts several lines from ear to ear across the forehead, often pressing so hard he incises the bone itself. Thereafter, it is clear to all not only that the boy has become a man, but also that he is a Nuer.[17]

In terms of social organization, the boys who were initiated in the same year belong to a named group which unites all men of similar age within the tribe, regardless of lineage or subtribal affiliation. A Nuer age set is in no way a military group. Men organize on other principles to fight. Individuals do enjoy special relationships within the set, though, having the obligation to give hospitality to one another and to share possessions. These pan-tribal associations do not dampen aggression, but in the absence of fighting, they encourage amity.

Associations among the Nuer seem largely neutral as concerns war and peace. In other parts of Africa as well as elsewhere among tribal societies, they may organize aggression. Secret societies in West Africa, for example, in some places strike terror in the hearts of nonmembers because members practice human sacrifice and cannibalism. Initiates of the Leopard Society wear leopard skins and leave the clawing marks of the leopard when they strike in the night to snatch a victim. But mostly, the associations of tribes organize for less dramatic purposes. Military associations among Plains Indians, for example, did not undertake raids. They were military in the sense that they recruited as members men who had fought successfully. On the whole, they functioned on the plains as much to maintain the peace as to encourage war.

Among some plains tribes, associations were age graded. Grown boys pursuing adult status bought rights to membership in the lowest of associations as each found a member willing to sell his ceremonial regalia and the right to dance certain dances and sing certain songs. Members selling to neophytes would themselves purchase new memberships in the next higher association. Thus, each association was largely made up of men of one age level. Age grading was not complete in many cases, because some individuals fell behind in buying and selling memberships. But on the whole, age sets were more formal in some plains tribes than among the Nuer, where membership is given less ritual reaffirmation.

Although associations were age graded in some plains tribes, in others they were not. Common to all, however, was the existence of various men's groups, each of which erected its own tent where members had a place to relax, sleep, eat, dance, sing, and chat. Typically, too, each association from time to time put on a public performance of its special dances for the entertainment of the encampment and as a claim to prestige.

Most importantly, these associations played an important role in war and peace. In one way, they encouraged war. Their songs and dances generally paid tribute to the ferocious warrior. A member of the kit-fox association of the Oglala Dakota tribe, for example, sang "I am a Fox: I am supposed to die. If there is anything difficult, if there is anything dangerous, that is mine to do."[18] Officials of the association had distinguished records of bravery and leadership in war. They epitomized the brave warrior. Oglala kit-fox leaders, for example, might paint their bodies yellow and carry lances in the kit-fox dance as a sign they had vowed not merely to lead a raid but to refuse to retreat, even in the face of death.

Associations encouraged the war ethic, but they did not normally organize fights. Just the contrary; in many tribes, their most important and regular function was to keep the peace. Among the Crow, the chief would designate a particular society each year to act as police during the hunting season. Among the Mandan, black mouth association membership included police duties. But whether rotated among societies or always the prerogative of one, in many tribes, the association and its officers took responsibility for good behavior during a march, at a tribe-wide meeting for the Sun Dance ceremony, or when large buffalo herds were in the vicinity. In the last case, it was essential that all men hunt as a unit. If some foolhardy or selfish individual tried to bag an animal by himself, he might scare off animals needed to keep the whole tribe alive.

Associations could enforce internal peace on these occasions by beating malefactors, sometimes so badly that bones were broken. In serious cases, they might even destroy a man's horses, tepees, and weapons. But such sanctions could be applied only within the encampment. Beyond the locality, which might include much of the tribe for a big hunt or dance, associations were helpless. A local association was never in a position to enforce peace between separated hostile camps or different tribes. Mechanisms for peace broke down on the plains as in the Sudan when they were extended beyond parochial boundaries.

On the whole, tribal social organization was ineffective in coping with war and peace because rational control was possible only on the local level. The result appears to have been endemic warfare. Rarely could a tribe avoid fighting. Even if it was distasteful to its own people, it was essential to survival, because neighbors were predatory. A vicious circle was the result. Tribes had to be aggressive because their neighbors were. A peaceful tribe in most places was doomed to extinction. Further, since fighting was necessary for survival, societies were better able to survive if they raised children with aggressive personalities. And so we find not merely that status is given to brave warriors, but that children are raised to value fortitude and toughness. Fierce personalities were encouraged, and fierce personalities generally thrived.

The whole tribal way of life, then, became oriented toward violence. The values espoused were warlike, and the social structure made the social expression of these values possible. But perhaps the ultimate cost of such a cultural system was the impact it had on personality development. Among the Nuer, for example, children are taught from infancy to settle their quarrels by fighting. As they get larger, boys find that the most prized accomplishments are skill in weaponry and courage in the face of danger. As adults, they tend to be vain, sensitive, and quick to anger. Much the same could be said for personality development among Plains Indians and, indeed, elsewhere. People who find cruelty and brutality congenial are the predictable product of tribal patterns of warfare. An internalized propensity to violence is widely found among tribal peoples. And to the extent that civilizations built upon Neolithic foundations, violence is the heritage of the modern world.

# 5  Noah's Curse

When the floodwaters receded and dry land appeared, Noah set forth from the ark with his three sons, Shem, Ham, and Japheth. In biblical tradition, all living peoples descend from these three sons. Further, an early episode involving Noah and his sons offers a biblical explanation for the fact that some people live as a favored class that enjoys the benefits of wealth, power, and leisure while most live in servitude.

It seems that Ham greatly offended Noah one day when the old man got blind drunk, so Noah put a curse on Canaan, the son of Ham, and presumably that curse was passed on to his descendants in perpetuity. "Cursed be Canaan," old Noah said; "a slave of slaves shall he be to his brothers."

The phrase "a slave of slaves" implies the existence of a higher level of slavery, and perhaps that was meant to indicate the future of the sons of Japheth, for Noah seemed to have intended him to occupy some sort of dependent position when he said, "let him dwell in the tents of Shem."

Shem, of course, was the lucky one. "Blessed by the Lord my God be Shem, and let Canaan be his slave." Shem and his descendants were destined to profit from the labors of slaves and the slaves of slaves. They were destined to form that elite that we designate loosely as an aristocracy or a ruling class.

The archeological record appears to confirm the antiquity of class-divided societies, and places their origin a few centuries before 3000 B.C.[1]

In Mesopotamia and Egypt at that time, the first Bronze Age cities were built. Civilization appeared, in the sense that societies with urban centers and elite cultures emerged. In subsequent millennia, early towns grew up in India, China, Middle America, and Africa.

With the passage of time, cities, nations, and empires took shape in various parts of the world. While some were growing to moments of greatness, others declined to extinction or had not yet begun their historic venture. With time, too, technological and political complexity progressed, so that early towns seem small and simple in later comparison. Since the latter part of the eighteenth century, industrialization has further complicated the picture. Social institutions and the quality of life are very different on either side of this historic watershed.

The rise and fall of civilizations constitute a historical maze. Yet for all their variability and change, preindustrial states and modern nations are of a kind in some ways. Compared with earlier and simpler societies, they are sociologically complex. They have urban and rural components. Generally they incorporate ethnic and ecological variety as well. Most importantly, they are divided into different social classes.

Classes can and often do occur in tribal societies. But tribal class systems generally are associated with relatively minor cultural differences among men. Further, the exploitation of one class by another does not normally proceed so far that one man can freeze or starve while another has more food and clothing than he needs. With civilizations, class divisions came to have a more profound effect on the quality of life for individuals. Men, who in the Neolithic had learned to domesticate animals, in the Bronze Age learned to domesticate other men. Class divisions so great that the lives of exploiters and exploited became very different are indicative of civilizations. This fact, admittedly, makes an irony of the term "civilization."

It is customary to speak of class structure in terms of differential access to political power, variability in the control and use of wealth, and different styles of life. Classes do differ in these ways. Yet perhaps no difference is more significant for the way people live than that which concerns the generation and expression of aggressive, hostile activity. With complex societies, the place of warfare in the scheme of life changed greatly from what it had been at the tribal stage.

Marshall D. Sahlins draws attention to this change in the quality of life. "In its broadest terms," he writes, "the contrast between tribe and civilization is between War and Peace." Continuing, he points out, "A civilization is a society specially constituted to maintain 'law and order'; the social complexity and cultural richness of civilizations depend on institutional guarantees of peace."[2]

Warfare, however, did not end with the appearance of complex societies. It continued to be endemic. The Harvard sociologist Pitirim Sorokin concluded from his study of eleven preindustrial nations in Europe that on the average a nation was involved in war nearly every other year.[3] Warfare remained common in earlier civilizations, just as it has in our own time. A few years ago, when Sweden celebrated its 150th year without war, that nation dramatized by its success that normally not a generation is born that does not experience the horror of war. Although warfare did not end with the appearance of complex, Bronze Age societies, it was turned to a new purpose. It became the instrument of elite minorities for subjugating the sons of Ham and Japheth.

When the Bronze Age emerged in Eurasia it made available new achievements in weaponry. Bronze swords, knives, and spears were superior to those of stone, bone, and wood. The horse was domesticated and harnessed to the war chariot. These new achievements were not equally available to all able-bodied men, however. Bronze was a scarce material.[4] It required skilled labor to be smelted and worked. Often the raw ore was not locally available, and could be had only through trade and travel. As a consequence, only a small number of men got the new weapons.

Those who got superior weapons gained the means to dominate their fellows. A warrior aristocracy was created, an elite of men who alone were equipped to fight others of their kind and who alone were able to subjugate those they defeated. Bronze Age principalities, city-states, and nations emerged in Mesopotamia and Egypt, northern India, and northern China. In southern Mexico and Guatemala as well as in Peru and neighboring regions, warrior elites also emerged, though the weapons were different and chariots unknown. In both the New World and the Old, power and wealth became concentrated in the hands of a small upper class.

Civilizations, then, grew as the social structure incorporated exploitative class relationships which permitted a small elite to monopolize power and wealth. As rulers and landlords, a dominant minority commandeered the surpluses of agrarian production to support non-food producers. Artisans produced the many goods which rich people enjoy. Priests elaborated upon religious ritual, and in devoting themselves to theology created science and literature as well. Governmental officials planned enterprises which kept their scribes hard-pressed to keep pace. Writing had become essential to the maintenance of new cultural standards. The aristocracy put the talents of men to the service of a more exciting, more comfortable, and more artistic life for the dominant class. But the aristocracy also used these resources to fight wars.

Aristocrats in preindustrial nations typically have been warriors. Of course, they may also have cultivated genteel arts, and at times, militarism receded. But ultimately, the privileges of the elite class rested upon the control of arms. The Samurai of Japan, the Mogul aristocrats in India, the Inca nobility in ancient Peru, Charlemagne and his men—all were the creators and supporters of civilized achievement. But they were professional fighters as well.

In the Old World, iron began to replace bronze after around 1400 B.C.— it did not reach the New World until the Spanish Conquest. When iron workers learned to make steel blades, the efficiency of war materiel increased. Organizational techniques improved too. In the last centuries of the old era, highly effective armies could be fielded and supplied, transported on wide-ranging ships in some cases. The Persian and Roman empires epitomized the success of new fighting systems. By the Middle Ages, gunpowder and stirruped horses further increased man's efficiency in killing, although such attainments pale in comparison with twentieth century advancements.

From the Bronze Age to the twentieth century, one feature of warfare remained essentially unchanged. Unlike tribal societies, fighting was largely the profession, or at least under the control of a small, dominant class. Ordinary people, but particularly peasants, often had their homes and communities destroyed, their bodies crippled or their lives snuffed out, their fields scorched and their time wasted. Yet rarely were they warriors, even when they fought. In that regard, they resembled more the horses that carried their masters than the masters as such. Like horses, they were domesticated, and like horses, they could be turned to work fields or fight battles as circumstances required.

The place of aggression in the lives of men changed, then, with the appearance of complex societies. For an elite, it remained prominent, and for an elite, the arrogance, the pride, the touchy sense of honor, and the brutality of warriors anywhere remained more or less characteristic. But for the masses, warfare had become something more akin to a natural calamity than a way of life. Like a typhoon or a severe drought, the call to arms or the passage of an army might bring misery to a village. But villagers in most places, even those who once had been drafted to fight, remained nonbelligerent in values and attitudes. Peasants concerned themselves with their fields and its produce, harvests and children, shelter and clothing, enough food to eat, and the celebration of family and community events in as joyful a manner as possible.

Peasant norms and values differed distinctively from those of warriors, and their personalities differed correspondingly. Although there are some exceptions, the peasant was not typically arrogant. In most places he was better characterized as subservient, obedient, taciturn, withdrawn, perhaps even obsequious. Too much under the control of powerful landlords to be otherwise, he had learned, like the cattle and sheep of his own herds, to do the bidding of his masters without resistance.

In agrarian nations, the vast majority of individuals are peasants. They normally constitute roughly 80 to 85 percent of the total population. Perhaps 5 or 10 percent of the total belong to the dominant class. The rest are mostly artisans, traders, and serving folk of various sorts whose life styles are as humble as that of the peasant even though they are different.

With the Industrial Revolution, a growing percentage of the population joined a new class, that of workers or proletarians. As peasants decreased in numerical importance, their place to a great extent was taken by the new working class. Working men, in the days before popular education and high wages, were as domesticated as peasants. In our own time, many countries still have peasantries and illiterate, underpaid work forces. Other deprived minorities also persist, including various racial and ethnic groups. The past is still very much with us in that sense.

In complex societies, the cost of militarism is great. That cost exceeds the carnage of wars fought and the brutalization of men who fight, grave as those are. Far more serious, without doubt, is the indirect consequence of militarism, the domination of common people by a small minority, the domestication of men by men. This cost is obscured because under traditional circumstances such minorities were the creators and perpetuators of civilizations. It was they who brought about the marvels of Han China, the glories of Egypt, the achievement of the Mayas in Mexico-Guatemala, the splendor of Rome, and other peaks in man's climb from simple beginnings. Without their work and success, the history of man would seem unfulfilled in retrospect, like a mother who remained forever pregnant. One cannot merely dismiss such elites in a gesture of revolutionary contempt. Yet one must look to the foundations as well as the tops of civilizational edifices. These structures were erected by common men—generally peasants—whose lives were impoverished to make greatness possible.

What does it mean to be a peasant? Romantic notions abound. They are in fact a product of the romanticism of the nineteenth century, when developing nations belatedly discovered their own folk heritages. It became popular to resuscitate folk art, folk music, folk dress, and folk literature. But even as that was happening, the peasantry was modernizing. In more traditional times, in the preindustrial period, rustic arts were not widely appreciated, and within villages themselves were not the pristine products of little utopias.

Peasants were parochial. Their ignorance was abysmal. Like zoo animals in cages, peasants had very little to challenge and stimulate emotions and intellect. They worked endlessly at the monotonous tasks of preparing and cultivating fields. Generally they were so heavily taxed, tithed, or charged that after the harvest they had only enough to live on—sometimes not that much, sometimes more. Sickness and death stood as perennial spectators of a treadmill existence alleviated only by the highlights of dull lives: the celebrations of weddings, funerals, and holy days.

For centuries, generation begat generation to survive in culturally pallid surroundings. That is our heritage today, and it raises an important question. We need to know if in breeding peasants and other deprived enclaves we have nurtured the seeds of our own destruction. At a time when the masses do or may control nations, the quality of their minds, their racial heritage, becomes a matter of tremendous importance. Having nurtured cow-like men, do we now have men with cow-like minds? The question of modernizing peasants is often raised. It is raised even more often for racial and ethnic minorities. Is the untouchable in India, the Korean in

Japan, the Indian in Mexico, or the Negro in America an inferior kind of man? Sometimes it is said he is. Often it is thought so. What are the facts?

One fact is that individuals from the peasantry and from ethnic or racial minorities often perform poorly on intelligence tests. In the United States, many surveys have found that Negroes and American Indians measure much lower than do whites. The recent work of Arthur Jensen indicates that the average I.Q. for American Negroes is 15 points lower than the average for American whites. Further, only 15 percent of the black population exceeds the average for whites. Where this really makes a difference is in the implications such measures are taken to have for capacity to succeed in higher education. Dr. Jensen takes an I.Q. of 115 as the minimum to get into college. Sixteen percent of whites score well enough by this measure to be educable at that level, but only the top 3 percent of the Negro population can make it.[5]

Some races measure as mentally inferior to others. What of peasants who are not distinguished by race? It can be argued that even where racial differences are not very obvious, true genetic inequality can be present. In testing done early in the present century in the United States, Poles and Italians, largely peasant in origin, scored significantly lower on intelligence tests than did individuals from northern Europe where industrialism has been present for the longest time.[6] Peasants, like racial minorities, score relatively low on intelligence tests. Does this indicate that they are biologically inferior as concerns brain development and potential?

As concerns Negroes in the United States, Arthur Jensen has argued that 80 percent of the difference between blacks and whites is due to heredity—that the measured inferiority is primarily genetic—and that it is therefore hopeless to attempt to educate most blacks at the college level or above, because they simply do not have the necessary mental equipment. The conclusion that Negroes or other deprived groups are inherently inferior, however, is wrong, and this can be demonstrated in a number of ways.

The Jensen study errs first of all in basic statistical technique. In order to compute the relative influence of environment as opposed to heredity, Jensen worked out a heritability index involving an analysis of variance. This means that he made judgments about the importance of various influences and weighted them numerically in order to be able to manipulate his judgments statistically. The weak link in this work is the subjectiveness of these numerical weightings. They involve, for example, assigning exact numerical values to variables such as the effect of a ghetto environment on a child's mind. The values assigned clearly are subject to distortion by personal and nonscientific beliefs. Martin Deutsch and his colleagues have identified seventeen instances in which Jensen made judgments of this sort which subjectively favored his thesis.[7] Remove these judgmental biases and you remove the statistical basis for concluding that it is heredity rather than personal milieu which results in differential scoring. In other words, do not let the statistics fool you. Behind them lie judgments which are inexact and subject to prejudicial distortion.

We must dismiss Jensen's conclusions as statistically distorted on the question of heredity versus environment. Yet we still have those differences in intelligence scores. How can you account for them?

Differences in I.Q. ratings appear to be the product of cultural impoverishment. Ghettos and peasant villages do not educate individuals to perform well on I.Q. tests, so they score low. Negroes perform significantly below whites on tests administered to people living in the American South. But in places in which blacks are few in number, are subjected to less severe forms of discrimination, and are educated in nonsegregated classes, they perform on the same level as whites.[8] The problem is social and cultural, not biological. Negroes in the United States—and deprived populations anywhere—typically grow up and are educated under circumstances which do not equip them to perform well on intelligence tests because the tests are designed, in effect if not in intent, to measure the achievement of middle class school children and educated adults.

It appears that racial and class differences in I.Q. scores are the product of social and cultural differences. This conclusion finds support in what we now know of racial biology. It seems clear that no living race is genetically inferior in brain development to any other. Demonstrating this point, however, requires careful attention to the dynamics of racial evolution. Above all, it requires an understanding of what race is, for perhaps no other subject in anthropology is more commonly misunderstood.

Because Africans, Chinese, Europeans, and others differ so obviously in physical appearance, it has long been customary to think of the human species as divisible into several major races. Fundamental to this conclusion is the assumption that an original number of races has remained essentially permanent and immutable for a very long time. Where people meet and interbreed, they mix but do not destroy the original racial types, so that primeval racial components can always be identified.

Generally, three to five basic races have been identified. This was true in the eighteenth century, when J. F. Blumenbach found a skull from the Caucasus which he felt epitomized the pure type of the European, and thus coined the term "Caucasian" (hence Caucasoid) for the white race.[9] It was true in 1948 when A. L. Kroeber wrote in terms of three grand divisions or primary stocks.[10] It is true in our time as Carleton S. Coon argues that the five modern races or subspecies, which he terms Australoid, Mongoloid, Caucasoid, Congoid [African Negro] and Capoid [Bushman], evolved from five equally distinct subspecies of *Homo erectus*.[11] This persistent and generally popular view of racial history as the odyssey of a small number of human types fails, however, to stand up under the scrutiny of modern science.

It is astonishing, really, how scientists have been biased by the folklore of race. Note the naive assumptions that racial reconstructions have forced us to accept. They force us to assume that races on the whole maintained their purity over many millennia when ample opportunities were present for interbreeding. Further, they force us to assume that where interbreeding did take place, it was sufficiently recent or limited to allow identification of the original racial ancestors.

This kind of naiveté led Earnest A. Hooton, in his classic reconstruction of man's racial history, to some more or less bizarre conclusions. His Indo-Dravidian "composite race" is illustrative. He described it as "predominantly White," but in sum, "Classic Mediterranean + Australoid (Veddoid) + Negrito + minor fractions of Iranian Plateau or Armenoid, Nordic, Mongoloid."[12] Count them! He claims to recognize elements of six races or subraces in the makeup of these people. Worse, the component parts are themselves mixed. If the Indo-Dravidian is not in part Iranian Plateau, then it is in part Armenoid, which is itself part Iranian Plateau. Ultimately, Hooton ends up talking in circles. The Australoid, a minor fraction of Indo-Dravidian, is also one of the morphological types of Indo-Dravidian.

The mistake in such evolutionary analysis is to assume that a race persists and has long persisted as a total biological entity. The facts do not support such assumptions. What are reported as major races generally are defined in terms of only a few traits. Professor Kroeber's criteria were skin color, hair form and color, eye color, head shape (cephalic index), nose shape (nasal index), and stature. But even these criteria are incompletely applied. The resultant racial categories really amount to no more than old folk races—red, yellow, brown, black, and white—but made respectable with fancier names.

Such classifications obscure the fact that bodily traits other than one or a few are quite variable within each race. Variations in the shape of the head, for example, or in stature, both used as sorting criteria by Kroeber, run from one extreme to the other, or very nearly so, within each of Kroeber's primary stocks. You can find long heads and round heads, tall and short individuals (though not pygmies) among Caucasoids, Mongoloids, and Negroids. Major races, in short, are merely statements about one or a small number of physical traits. They are not, as supposedly they are, complete statements about group heredity. When they do approach being complete statements, they cease to apply to large populations, or they apply to one of several with recent histories which have resulted in unusual homogeneity of body type.

The Mongoloid race is normally thought of as characterized by the following traits: straight, coarse black hair; yellow or yellow-brown skin color;

medium to dark brown eyes; a slit-like, slanting eye opening shaped by a heavy, fat-embedded upper lid which forms a fold (the epicanthus); a low-rooted, low-bridged nose of medium breadth displaying a concave or straight profile; cheek bones with a strong frontal and lateral jut, usually covered with a fat pad, and very little beard or body hair. This description, in fact, is drawn directly from Hooton's sorting criteria for what he terms the Mongoloid primary race.[13]

But these traits do not describe all members of the Mongoloid race. They do not describe the Indonesian Mongoloid or the American Indian Mongoloid or the Malay Mongoloid. They are, in fact, descriptive of the Chinese, who once were merely a local ethnic stock around the middle reaches of the Yellow River, but who have expanded in number during recent millennia and have pushed in all directions to cover most of what is now China as well as areas beyond. In their expansion, the Chinese have replaced, mated with, assimilated or greatly outnumbered indigenous peoples who until the expansion were different ethnically and racially. The Mongoloid race as generally thought of, then, covers China, Japan, and other parts of mainland Asia, yet is largely the product of family-like resemblances in a population which has spread widely in relatively recent times from a small original homeland.

The same is true of other major races. The classic Negroid, with woolly or frizzly black hair, dark brown to black skin color, broad nose, and everted lips, is widespread in Africa and elsewhere today.[14] Yet these traits were once largely characteristic of Bantu-speaking peoples in a small part of western central Africa. The Bantu, like the Chinese, though later in time, expanded in population and pushed outward to replace, displace, or assimilate indigenous peoples. Many, of course, eventually ended up in other parts of the world through slave trading. The Negroid race as commonly defined, then, is not an ancient, pure, and largely unchanging biological type. It is a type which, in its classic definition, only recently has become widespread.

Caucasoids, for their part, appear to have moved from their home in the Middle East, largely within the last 5,000 years. They spread first as an expanding population of Neolithic cultivators, pushing out the small, scattered societies of hunters that had preceded them. Their spread increased in size and density with the appearance of the first expanding archaic states.

In the New World, such expansions of Neolithic and civilized societies were late and less pervasive in effect. Correspondingly, the American Indian is rather variable in type, and generally not distinguished by the widespread occurrence of unusual features such as the everted lip, the Mongoloid fold, or blondism. If Indians seem similar throughout the hemisphere, it is largely because they do not display the extremes of pigmentation or structure which in other parts of the world diffused as relatively recent historical events. This absence of specialized traits has made it seem reasonable to consider them Mongoloid, though clearly without the distinctive features of Asiatic Mongoloids.

What do we conclude from these observations? We do not conclude that races do not exist. Clearly, we can distinguish Mongoloids, Negroids, Caucasoids, and others. But such races now appear to be either groups distinguished mainly by one or a few traits, or widespread body types produced by historical processes essentially the same as those which produce similar looking individuals within a reproductively successful family. When relatively recent descent from common ancestors is explanatory, the resemblances can be expected to decrease with time. This is just the opposite of what is generally assumed about racial types. So races exist. But they mean very little compared to what they are assumed to mean in popular and even in much scientific thought.

Because races have proved to be essentially ephemeral rather than stable and pure, some anthropologists are arguing that it is best to discard the very notion of race. Frank B. Livingstone in recent years has written "On the Nonexistence of Human Races,"[15] and Ashley Montagu agrees, but more colorfully, as he writes that "The process of averaging the characters of a given group, knocking the individuals together, giving them a good stirring, and then serving the resulting omelet as a 'race' is essentially the anthropological process of race-making. It may be good cooking," Dr. Montagu points out, "but it is not science, since it serves to confuse rather than to clarify."[16]

The dominant feature of human evolution is not racial formation but a very different process best characterized as discordant variation. That is, physical traits do not tend to vary together, to cluster (concordant variation) but tend to be largely independent of one another as one traces them from population to population (discordant variation). It is discordance, not concordance, which makes sense in terms of genetic theory and which best accounts for human body types. At this juncture, it is appropriate to glance briefly at the theorizing of Charles Darwin.

The achievement of Darwin was not to realize for the first time that man is the product of biological evolution rather than of some special creative act. Others had that idea before him. Darwin's contribution was to indicate for the first time what the process of evolutionary development might be. He proposed the notion of natural selection. It works like this. In any species, more offspring are produced in any generation than can survive. These offspring vary somewhat in hereditary composition. Some may be slightly better able to survive than others in what Darwin termed the struggle for existence. It is the advantaged ones who will be the most likely to grow to adulthood and to have offspring themselves. In Darwin's terms, the result will be the survival of the fittest. Since the process is repeated among offspring as one generation follows another, eventually better adaptive traits will replace those which are less adaptive in the population.

Since races by most definitions cover rather large and environmentally diverse areas, it is unrealistic to assume that natural selection works uniformly within such territorial expanses to produce the biological uniformity (the concordance) we imply by the term "race." The contrary is the case. Just as one part of the environment (for example, climate) has a different geographical distribution from another part (for example, altitude), so one body trait (for example, resistence to freezing) will have a different distribution from another (for example, resistance to altitude sickness). C. Loring Brace is among those who have especially stressed this point: *"The most important thing for the analysis of human variation is the appreciation of the selective pressures which have operated to influence the expression of each trait separately."*[17] In other words, different bodily traits have different geographical distributions, and the characteristics of any one population will place it in different groups depending upon which trait one takes as the sorting criterion. A few examples will make this clear.

Before exploration and colonization greatly changed the distribution of men over the face of the earth, dark skin color characterized most, but not all, people who lived within 15 or 20 degrees of the equator. Lighter-skinned peoples lived north or south of this band. Apparently, heavy pigmentation provides a selective advantage to individuals in a hot climate, perhaps because it hinders too high an intake of vitamin D, which is harmful in large amounts, and perhaps because it reduces the amount of ultraviolet radiation absorbed below the outer layer of the skin and thus offers protection against skin cancer. Other things being equal then, and for present purposes we can leave it at that, whether or not a population has dark skin depends upon location relative to the equator. Within the equatorial area, dark skin could be shared through genetic interchange as mating took place over social boundaries. But dark skin might also appear independently as separate populations responded in parallel fashion to similar selective features of the environment. No doubt dark skin has resulted from both processes. The end result is the same.[18]

The shape of the face has a rather different distribution from that of skin color.[19] In part, facial form is a reflection of tooth size, and only that need concern us here. Large teeth are associated with a large lower face. Tooth (and face) shape is quite unresponsive to climate as such, however. It can vary independently of the equator. Rather, tooth size appears to display an inverse relationship with technological complexity. In brief, hunting and gathering peoples, with simple tools, use their incisors as tools and their mouths as third hands. Witness the Eskimo, who softens leather by chewing, steadies his bone drill with his teeth, and in many other ways depends upon his mouth as a hand. The result is heavy wear on teeth.

The genetically selective pressure is for larger, stronger incisors in technologically simple (hunting and gathering) societies. And what we find, in short, is that the distribution of tooth size, and to that extent, facial form, corresponds to the distribution of Neolithic and civilizational development. Quite unbound by "race," the smallest teeth and the smallest faces are to be found along a broad band extending across Europe, the Near East, northern India, the Far East and Southeast Asia, places in which the population earliest became Neolithic in culture. (The evidence for the New World is not good, but apparently the smallest teeth occur in the areas of highest civilizational development, Middle America.) Conversely, the biggest teeth and largest lower faces are to be found among living hunting peoples or where hunting survived the longest. Dr. Brace sums up his findings by stressing that "the distribution of dental size bears no relation to that of skin color since the important influencing forces vary quite independently."[20]

Races, in major part commonly delimited in terms of skin color, are meaningless concepts for understanding facial form. They are equally meaningless for still other characteristics. The trait for a condition of the red blood cells known as sickle-cell anemia further illustrates this conclusion.[21] Sickle-cell anemia, though it has disadvantages, has a powerful selective advantage in certain areas. It is associated with immunity to malaria. Whether through independent development or interbreeding, the trait has an Old World distribution which cuts across traditional racial boundaries. It does not occur in major parts of Africa, Europe, or Asia, yet it is found among Negroids in West Africa and among Caucasoids in North Africa, southern Europe, the eastern Mediterranean, and parts of the Near East. In India and Burma it occurs among people classifiable as Mongoloid. Its distribution seems determined, in sum, by the presence or absence of malaria, and similarities in this trait are the product, presumably, of either gene diffusion through interbreeding or parallel development in two or more places or a combination of both.

Robert D. McCracken recently provided us with another example of independent variation.[22] His concerns the adult capacity to produce the enzyme lactase. All infants have this capacity, since it is essential for the successful assimilation of milk. But adults may become deficient in lactase production, and thus unable to digest the lactose of milk. For such individuals, drinking milk results in bowel distension, cramps, gas, and diarrhea.

Distribution of the presence or absence of lactase production in adults is instructive. Thus far in his studies, Dr. McCracken has found only two populations in which adults typically have this capacity to produce lactase, and thus to consume whole milk. They are European whites with their descendants and the Nilotic Negroes of East Africa. Conversely, populations in which the majority of adults are lactase-deficient consists of other Negroes (including American), Australian aborigines, Chinese, American Indians,

New Guinea Islanders, Filipinos, and Thais. The distribution of this enzyme characteristic varies independently of generally accepted racial boundaries. It appears to vary as a genetic correlate of a cultural variable. Lactase deficiency is common in populations which have never practiced dairying or which, like the Thais, Chinese, Filipinos, and most African Negroes, raise cattle but do not consume raw milk. But in those populations which since the inauguration of the Neolithic have incorporated milk consumption into their diet, selectivity apparently has favored individuals who persisted beyond childhood in producing this critical enzyme.

Distribution studies of individual traits, then, lead to a conclusion. The dominant trend of human evolution is not to create uniform races. It is to result in largely independent assortments of traits, a process in which different bodily characteristics respond more or less independently to different aspects of the environment (including culture). The product is differential geographical distributions for different traits.

Races as generally defined are shadowy, badly delineated entities on the whole. They do not ordinarily indicate members' stature, head shape, facial form, blood type, enzyme capabilities or other inherited features. This is unequivocally clear for easily measured physiological and anatomical traits. But what of intelligence?

Intelligence defies objective measurement as we have seen. But from what we now know of racial processes, we can draw a highly significant inference about mental ability. Where selective pressures favor intelligence, we would expect the evolutionary process to have led to an increased mental capacity. Conversely, where selective pressures are either neutral for intelligence or select negatively, we would expect intelligence to be reduced in quality. Selective forces rather than measured intelligence can be our guide. And what do we find? I think it is abundantly clear that as far as general intelligence is concerned every human society, whether prehistoric or contemporary, has selected for high mental ability.

Human life everywhere demands a well-developed capacity for rapid adjustment to complex and changing circumstances. "Suppleness, plasticity, and, most important of all, ability to profit by experience and education are required," write Theodosius Dobzhansky and Ashley Montagu.[23] From this it follows that these intellectual capacities have survival value, and therefore will tend to develop through natural selection.

> In the ordinary course of events in almost all societies those persons are likely to be favored who show wisdom, maturity of judgment, and ability to get along with people—qualities which may assume different forms in different cultures. Those are the qualities of the plastic personality, not a single trait but a general condition, and this is the condition which appears to have been at a premium in practically all human societies.[24]

Among hunters, the slightly more intelligent man has an advantage in improving his knowledge of the ways of animals and how to kill them, as well as in cooperating with other men for this purpose. He can be expected to be more successful in the hunt. And even though such superiority may be very slight in any particular instance, in critical times mentally superior men will be more likely to survive to adulthood, more likely to get and keep wives, and, the ultimate genetic test, more likely to have offspring who will themselves be favored for survival. Darwin's natural selection works for intelligence as for any other inherited trait. Further, uniform selectivity in favor of intelligence has not declined with time. Even deprived peasants or Negro slaves may be expected to select for greater intelligence. The slightly more intelligent peon is slightly more likely to be successful in growing food, in calculating his risks, in negotiating with his masters.

Over many millennia, men must have slowly but surely bred for intelligence everywhere. On the level of continents and subcontinents, of centuries and millennia of time, I can imagine no area where, through genetic interchange or parallel development, men did not breed for intelligence as surely as they uniformly bred for bipedal posture, efficient hand-eye coordination, and other species-wide capabilities. Individuals within a group vary in intelligence. Among our acquaintances, we all know individuals who are bright and others who are not. But the range is undoubtedly the same for all populations. In every population, selectivity has been the same in this regard.

All that we presently know of racial processes leads to the conclusion that the races are equally endowed in general intelligence. In class-stratified societies, however, the intellectual equality of populations may be obscured by psychological barriers. The work of George DeVos and Hiroshi Wagatsuma on the low caste Burakumin of Japan is particularly instructive in this regard.[25]

Most people are not aware that a minority population lives in Japan which is as discriminated against as Negroes have been in the United States. Their presence is disguised by the fact that they are relatively few in number, but also that they are racially indistinguishable from the majority population. DeVos and Wagatsuma, in fact, refer to them as "Japan's invisible race." Yet they exist, and they are regarded as dirty, diseased, immoral, and dangerous. It is this negative attitude toward the Burakumin which seems to explain their failure in many instances to succeed better in contemporary Japan. An invidious evaluation apparently functions as a self-fulfilling prophesy.

DeVos and Wagatsuma stress the effects of discrimination on personality development. "Minority status requires an individual to cope continually with a negative self-image automatically internalized as he becomes socialized in a disparaging majority society," they write.[26] In an interview with a Burakumin who passes during the day as a city official in Osaka, they were told that a Burakumin can be recognized, even though his race is not different, simply because he bears the marks of poor housing, bad sanitation, brutal work, dirty food, crude language, rough behavior, and laziness. This man's own low evaluation of his own "invisible race" is instructive. He sees Burakumin—and hence himself—as suffused by "something vicious, something dirty, something unnameable, but something which can be felt, like a strong odor." The informant goes on to say, "This something horrible permeates or gets into the people who are born and raised and live in this area. It is something like a bad body odor."[27] The result is, even in the absence of a color bar to self-advancement, members of the despised group cannot easily break out of their deprived condition. They are held back, not by biological inferiority, but by barriers which are social, cultural, and psychological in origin.

This leads to an important conclusion. Some populations do perform less successfully than others in achieving goals they all share as members of a modern civilization. Minority populations not only cannot get good-paying, ego-satisfying jobs, but when employed often do not succeed. Minorities not only cannot get good schooling, but when in school, often do not perform well. Minorities not only cannot often get into good neighborhoods, but when able to move in, frequently do not find contentment. The problems are very real. But the nature of the solution depends upon the source of the problem. There are two main possibilities. The problems could be entirely, largely, or at least partly genetic. In that case, the solution would be some sort of biological manipulation or certain kinds of biologically justified training and employment programs. But if the problems are entirely nonbiological, then the solutions are to be sought for in what we know and can find out about cultural processes.

As between these two alternatives, the answer is clear. Races and classes do not differ in general intellectual ability. Races do not even exist in this regard. Further, the domestication of men to create ethnic and racial minorities, including peasantries, has not resulted in reduced intellectual capacity. From all we know of poor performance in low-ranked populations, it seems clear that the source of differential performance is social discrimination, and that the way to eliminate discriminatory differences is to apply what we know of social, cultural, and psychological processes to this end. This still leaves us a very long way from the top of the mountain. But at least we can identify the right path to follow.

# 6  The Promised Land

Knowing something of what it means to be a peasant in Latin America, a black in South Africa, an untouchable in Asia, or a child of the ghetto in the United States, one can understand a desire to deliver the Israelites out of bondage in Egypt and bring them to a land flowing with milk and honey. For deprived peoples in our time, as in the time of Moses, there must be a Promised Land, the hope for a better future. In anthropology, we speak of that hope as a problem in culture change.

The Israelites suffered greatly in making the move from bondage in Egypt to freedom in the Promised Land. For 40 years they wandered in the wilderness. Men in our time are not so patient. They want change fast and they want it without decades of hunger and the oppressive burden of being humbled by the powers that be. Applied anthropology is concerned with this aspect of the problem, to help men reach the Promised Land as rapidly and easily as possible.

Civilized man set new standards for what was considered the good life. Whether in Middle America, the Far East, Europe, or Africa, impressive advances took place in art, architecture, literature, music, entertainment, knowledge, philosophy, and science. In different parts of the world, the style of such activities varied, but in centers of civilization everywhere, new heights were reached. Even though one's evaluation of such achievement is partly or even largely subjective, it is clear that never before had men so liberated the creative spirit.

Preindustrial civilizations set high standards for cultural enrichment. But its benefits were limited to a small elite class which held a monopoly on wealth and power. As the Industrial Revolution gained momentum in the eighteenth century and reached out to the present, the quality of civilizational achievement grew apace. Growing technological competence was harnessed to the cause. Rationally strained for perfection as science and technology gave new efficiency to the quest for inherited goals. Knowledge and achievement in our time dwarf their antique and medieval fathers. It is not entirely popular today to say such things, since many are disillusioned with modern life. Yet in the perspective of anthropology, a most important part of the present state of humanity is the level of twentieth century accomplishment.

In the modern world, the benefits of civilization have been extended to a more substantial part of the total population. Contemporary industry, with its infrastructure of governmental institutions and educational enterprises, supports a class of people who are paid enough for work in high-status occupations to allow them to be comparatively well fed, well housed, and well educated. In the West, as in the Third World, we characterize them as the middle class, while in communist nations they have been referred to as the new class, or they simply exist without official recognition, since according to Marxist ideology they should disappear in a socialist state.

In general, the middle classes have not been an inspiring lot. They have produced and supported men like Einstein and Shakespeare. They also have produced less gifted individuals who nonetheless have shown they could enrich their own lives and those of their contemporaries. Yet too often, as also was true of the old upper classes, the ordinary individual has been unimaginative, culture bound, and parochial. One of the most serious problems yet to be solved is how to create an affluent society in which individuals will strive for self-fulfillment rather than mere self-indulgence. Awareness of this problem, however, tends to diminish in the face of other, more pressing difficulties.

The masses of many nations and minorities in most suffer gross deprivation. Men and women and boys and girls still age and die prematurely from chronic hunger, sickness, and exhaustion. For them, the pleasures of life are not only few, but grasped at from the steep precipices of imminent personal catastrophe. Those more fortunate cannot truly know what such a life means, except as briefly, in a moment of satanic enlightenment, the mind's eye glimpses and then obliterates its misery.

Many who thus suffer do so as survivors of preindustrial civilizations, as peasants who till the soil under exploitative tenure arrangements, mired down by technologically backward equipment. Others, the new masses, cluster in towns and cities as unskilled and semiskilled laborers who are the urban poor.

The anthropological study of contemporary peoples has been uneven in the attention it has given to different kinds of society. Largely it has focused upon surviving band and tribal societies. Within civilizations, most work has been concentrated upon peasants. More recently, considerable attention has been given to the urban poor. Only a few have studied the middle classes and even fewer, the upper classes.

In the search for generalizations which can be made about each kind of society, a fundamental problem for many anthropologists in recent decades has been, what is peasant culture? Answers to this question are still not wholly satisfactory. "The peasant is an immemorial figure on the world social landscape," Clifford Geertz pointed out in 1962, "but anthropology noticed him only recently."[1]

George M. Foster is no doubt right to insist that the definitive criteria of peasantries are not occupational but structural and relational. That is, it is not that peasants rely upon agricultural production rather than, say, fishing, but rather that rural peoples have a particular kind of socioeconomic tie to a larger society which includes nonpeasants. According to Foster, "When settled rural peoples subject to the jural control of outsiders exchange a part of what they produce for items they cannot themselves make, in a market setting transcending local transactions, then they are peasants."[2] This, at least, would seem to distinguish them insofar as their culture remains substantially different from that of dominant or urban classes. When their culture becomes very similar to that of other classes, the peasants have become farmers, quite another class of people.

Robert Redfield, who pioneered in theorizing about peasants, hoped to compile a list of cultural features that would hold true all over the world. Early in his work, he felt he had found a cluster of three traits: "an intimate and reverent attitude toward the land; the idea that agricultural work is good and commerce not so good; and an emphasis on productive industry as a prime virtue."[3] He soon found, however, that for every generalization he made, other anthropologists could find exceptions. It is difficult to go beyond such regularities as are inherent in exploitative socioeconomic relationships with nonpeasants. Perhaps the fundamental shared characteristic is simply that, and what Eric R. Wolf has termed the peasant dilemma, the problem a peasant has of meeting his own individual, family, and communal needs when they are in conflict with what outsiders demand of him.[4] Characteristic of peasants everywhere is that they are different in their way of life from other classes, that they are rural, and that they have little control over wealth and power because they are subject to outsiders. Typically they are poor.

Oscar Lewis coined the phrase "culture of poverty." As he used it, it does not apply to peasants, for it is not meant to designate all people who are poor.[5] Rather, it constitutes a statement about urban slum dwellers in many parts of the world, though not in all. Poverty occurs everywhere, but the culture of poverty refers to a particular way of living with it. Documented for Eurasia and the Americas, it seems rare in Africa and absent in socialist nations. It is an urban way of life characterized by the absence of effective participation in major institutions other than jails, public welfare systems, and military conscription. On the local level, too, social participation is unorganized, in spite of crowding, and the gregariousness of neighbors. The result is that people live primarily in terms of the family. Yet family solidarity is weakened by informal or common law unions, frequent abandonment of wives and children, sibling rivalry, and competition within the family for money, food, and maternal attention. The result for the individual is apathy and fatalism, "a strong feeling of marginality, of helplessness, of dependence and of inferiority."[6] This is the culture of poverty.

In recent decades, cultural anthropologists have been moved by the need to understand the processes whereby deprived peoples, peasant, slum, or other, become participants in the benefits of civilization. The goal of raising standards of living among the urban poor, peasants, and other impoverished societies is not challenged by reasonable men. What is debated is how best to achieve this goal. So vast and important a project requires many different kinds of specialists to contribute their expertise. Economists, political scientists, health technicians, and politicians are only a few of those involved. Anthropologists very importantly are included. For all, however, because the problem is so supremely complex, the search for answers is still more or less immature. Anthropologists are only in the first stages of being able to contribute helpfully to an understanding of culture change in these circumstances.

In many ways, anthropologists have adopted what can be termed a cookbook approach to culture change. From observations in every part of the world, we offer a variety of experience, a collection of recipes for various problems in the form of guidelines or helpful hints. The work of George Foster offers many examples of this sort, including the following taken from his recent book *Applied Anthropology*.[7]

In Venezuela the government set up rural clinics which in part were to contribute to maternal and infant health by distributing free powdered milk.[8] Mothers, however, exchanged their allotments of milk for liquor and adult foods, so that they and their babies showed little nutritional improvement. How do you resolve a difficulty of this sort?

An anthropologist faced with such a problem would first question all concerned. In this instance, interrogation revealed that clinic technicians had failed to demonstrate good techniques for liquifying powdered milk and for combining it with foods agreeable to local tastes. But in addition, talks with the mothers revealed cultural attitudes which hindered. Feeding powdered milk to their babies was taken to imply a maternal incapacity to breast-feed properly. Also, it seemed unfair to them that their husbands and others in the family should not profit from the distribution, so they exchanged milk packages for other items. With such information, the solution was easy to find. As a new policy, milk cans were opened on distribution to prevent later exchange with storekeepers. In addition, a better integration of milk into the traditional diet was stimulated by the demonstration of food preparation techniques and prize awards. The program began to succeed.

In my own historical research on Eskimo economic development I encountered a serious problem in culture change.[9] In this case, Alaskan Eskimo were suffering from chronic starvation because commercial whaling had depleted Arctic waters of whale and walrus. A new food resource was to be developed by introducing domestic reindeer. Some Scandinavian Lapps were brought over to train Eskimo hunters in herding techniques.

With the passage of time, the enterprise fell far short of its original promise. Ranges were depleted by overgrazing. Herds were depopulated as animals were killed by wolves, ran off with wild caribou (with which they can mate), or died in accidents from lack of attention. With domesticated reindeer as a new food resource, wolves increased in numbers. The results were nearly disastrous.

To an inquiring anthropologist, the source of difficulty soon became apparent. At first, the Eskimo emulated the close-herding techniques of southern Lapps. But among the latter, this technique depends upon the watchful care of small herds which will support a family only if the animals are used for hauling sledges, milking for the production of cheese, and moving family and tents with the herds in the annual migration. Eskimos failed because they stayed in their settlements, overgrazed nearby pastures, did not milk, and continued to keep dogs for sledging. They thought they were emulating a successful Lapp system. Actually, they created a hybrid which was doomed to fail.

Later, the Eskimo shifted to the northern Lapp technique of open herding. Again, though, they failed to emulate a system which was successful in Scandinavia. Under this system, Lapp animals are raised in large herds for meat and skins. They are not milked, except for short periods each year, and a smaller percentage, but still a very important number, are used for hauling freight. The Eskimo, though, never milked. They still did not use reindeer for hauling. But worst of all, they mistook these extensive herding techniques for no herding at all. They left their animals to roam unattended. In part, this no doubt reflected their failure to appreciate the need for careful guarding. But in part, too, it reflected a deficiency in ownership arrangements. Lapp reindeer, though herded in large communal herds, belong to individuals. In the winter, each family separates its deer from the common herd. Because each deer is owned in this way, each individual feels a personal responsibility for the larger herd. The Eskimo organized their herding by establishing reindeer associations in which each person had a share in the profit. The arrangement supported no sense of individual ownership or commitment and made it easy for individuals to shirk their responsibilities. Once again, a hybrid was created that was destined to fail. To this day, the reindeer industry in Alaska has fallen short of ultimate success.

Applied anthropology, as seen in these examples and many others similar to them, is as much an art as a science at the present time. It draws upon a fortuitous but growing body of documentation in which systematic analysis is combined with simple experience. It relies heavily upon an open-ended approach to collecting information which draws directly upon the techniques of ethnography. Much of what it contributes is in the nature of fact finding. Beyond that, it typically draws attention to two major areas of potential difficulty.

One area of recurrent difficulty is that of cultural fit.[10] Powdered milk in Venezuela, for example, was not acceptable until it could be adjusted to traditional dietary habits and values, including the attitude that adults as well as children should profit from family resources. Among the Eskimo, much of the promise of reindeer herding resided in the good potential fit it had for an Alaskan hunting culture which was similar to that of prehistoric Lapps. The comprehensive approach of anthropology makes one especially alert to this dimension of the culture change problem.

The second broad area of potential difficulty which anthropologists are inclined to look for is that of communication.[11] We find that outside planners frequently do not know what is happening or how people in the target community are reacting to proffered innovations. Sometimes what they offer is not even useful to those they hope will adopt it. Conversely, potential adopters often do not understand the intent and potential advantages of proposed changes or how to accept what they want. In the Venezuelan and Alaskan examples, breakdown of communication at least partially explained the failure, just as improvement of communication offered some hope of success. In Venezuela, health experts and villagers had conflicting perceptions concerning the usefulness of powdered milk. In Alaska, the diffusion of herding techniques from Lapps to Eskimo broke down insofar as incorrect and incomplete transmission took place. Problems of communication, including perception of what is happening, clearly constitute a recurrent difficulty in culture change.

Communists and noncommunists alike want to raise living standards for workers and peasants. They disagree, of course, on the form of government and the desirable national values for achieving this aim. Eventually, beyond rhetoric, capitalist and communist ideologies get translated into action programs. Noncommunists support or permit cooperative movements, unionization, rural development programs, economic opportunities legislation, and technical assistance, whether in their own nations or in nations they wish to help. On the other side of the ideological curtain, communist nations support change organized by Communist Party cadres, factory management by workers, collectivization, or communalization.

At the level of action programs—of people at their work—one can better hope to evaluate the relative merits of the two strategies for change than at the level of social and political theory. At this level, one can examine efforts to implement the two strategies and judge the results, for the closer he gets to real individuals and concrete problems, the more objective he can be.

Immediately in this enterprise, a highly important statement must be made. In the process of guiding or managing culture change, serious ethical problems always arise. When planners decide to take action, they make decisions for people other than themselves. Anthropologists and others have found it important to draw attention to this, and to the potentialities such situations have for neglecting the rights and best interests of populations whose lives are affected.

Fundamentally, the ethical problem concerns the right all people ought to have to take part in decisions which concern them. In the noncommunist world, the problem is frequently thought of as involving the need to distinguish the modernization of cultures, something which probably is unavoidable, from westernization, which may be culturally imperialistic.

Villagers and workers in India, Latin America, Africa, or elsewhere must adopt modern technology and make related changes in their way of life if they are to survive. It happens that the Industrial Revolution first took place in Europe and America, so modernization comes dressed in Western clothes. Yet clearly, cultivators can adopt the steel plow without converting to Christianity, factory workers can regulate their lives by clock and calendar without scheduling in terms of a week of seven days; members of the middle class can incorporate new standards of bodily comfort without dressing in shirts and ties. In short, villagers, slum dwellers, and others can adopt new standards of living without giving up all traditional values.

This problem, however, is more complicated than appears at first appraisal. The challenge, in the words of the sociologist William McCord, is "to construct a society receptive to modernization without utterly destroying traditional civilizations."[12] In the process, however, one must be prepared to see traditional values greatly changed even as they survive. It is a mistake to assume that people can incorporate modern industrialism and yet remain quite unchanged in religious attitudes and practices, daily and annual scheduling, or even in housing and dress. Nearly every part of their lives may be affected.

Changing peoples need not slavishly imitate the West. People need not become Christians. But they may well need to adjust their religious thinking. As Chester L. Hunt has pointed out, "The tradition-bound rigidity of Islam, the otherworldly emphasis of Buddhism, the asceticism of Hinduism and the fiesta-laden Catholicism of countries with a Spanish tradition may embody important teachings, but their emphasis is not calculated to produce industrious workers, thrifty capitalists, or daring promoters."[13] Of course people may retain their ancestral religions. But those religions may need to be modified to accommodate new modes of conduct.

Again, in the pacing of life activities, rest days and holidays need not be set by the Christian calendar, with its emphasis on Sundays and Christmas. Yet a modern economy does require regularity in daily and annual work schedules. This demands great change in peasants and slum dwellers who normally work or rest as season, family commitment, and opportunity require. Timing in a natural economy is very different from what it is in an industrial economy. The man who puts off a task for tomorrow may succeed quite well as a peasant or even as a slum dweller. He will fail, however, in a modern business enterprise if he is not regularly at his job.

The chain reaction of adaptation may even extend into seemingly remote areas of culture. Dress, for example, may need to be redesigned. The West has clothes which meet modern needs. Others may not wish to imitate Western styles. Yet they will face pressure to exchange or modify flowing or constricting garments for new ones which free one for action yet do not offer dangerous edges to catch on moving vehicles and machinery. Those who wear little clothing may find they need to wear more for protection in factory work.

If you fly Air India today, you will be served by hostesses wearing the traditional flowing sari. In India in general, the sari still is worn. Yet one sees signs that it is threatened. As women now increasingly find employment in offices, factories, and shops, they find that their clothes catch on things and inhibit easy movement. I would not hope to predict the future of this form of dress. Its inconveniences are countered by the attractions of simplicity and good looks. But whether or not the sari survives will in part be determined by whether or not it is convenient in modern life, not simply by whether or not Indians want to emulate the West.

In sum, it is immoral to insist that modernizing people imitate the West in those customs which permit variation. But it is unreasonable to assume that people can avoid making many changes which will resemble at least generically those taken in the West. What is inevitable cannot be immoral.

The West does not have a monopoly on ethical problems in culture change. Under communism, the difficulty also arises, though there the problem generally is phrased differently by observers. Curiously, it tends to be forgotten that cultural imperialism is involved. In the West, planners alerted to the distinction between modernization and westernization are able ideologically and practically to encourage, support, or manage change without ethical abuse in this regard. Frequently, this has not been done, but it can be. Even Christian missionaries in recent years often have found it possible to focus upon educational, medical, or developmental objectives with little or no attempt to proselytize beyond the example a man gives in his own way of living.

But while it is possible for Western agents of change to cope with this sort of ethical difficulty, it is extremely difficult for communists. Their commitment to party goals is a commitment to replace traditional cultures with doctrinaire norms and values, to transform individuals, families, communities, and nations. Noncommunist nations have been guilty of cultural imperialism in many instances, but not in all, and thoughtful planners avoid it. Communist nations have nearly always been imperialistic in this sense, and they find it nearly impossible to do otherwise so long as they remain communists.

Communist planners have not been held to the same standards as others as regards cultural imperialism. But they have not gone unchallenged in the realm of ethics. Frequent and vociferous protests have drawn attention to the immorality of imposing change by force. The redistribution of land has typically been achieved by fiat. Landlords in China and their counterparts in Russia and elsewhere were rendered paupers overnight, and large numbers had their families broken up and were themselves tortured and killed. Peasants and workers who proved uncooperative or recalcitrant in the revamping of national life have been punished and disenfranchised with equal ruthlessness.

In the initial years of communist modernization, at the least, the pattern nearly everywhere has been to create new inequities in the process of wiping out the old. "To put it bluntly," Mao Tse-tung argued in 1927, "it was necessary to bring about a brief reign of terror in every rural area. . . . To right a wrong it is necessary to exceed the proper limits, and wrong cannot be righted without the proper limits being exceeded."[14] Anticommunists have at times been as ruthless as Mao in imposing "solutions" for culture change. Vietnam alone constitutes a heavy indictment of the United States. But in the Free World, many spokesmen argue that terror and "improper" behavior (the use of force) are unacceptable tactics for changing people. Among communists, spokesmen for that viewpoint normally have been silenced.

Culture change strategies can be evaluated in practical as well as ethical terms. Anthropologically, we can attempt to calculate the relative efficiency of communist and noncommunist techniques. We need to know, moral or not, whether communist tactics can work, just as we need to know the potentiality of noncommunist methods. We cannot evade the obligation to attempt to decide which is better in these terms.

It is difficult to compare strategies when the entities under analysis are designated only vaguely as communist or noncommunist. Russia, Cuba, Yugoslavia, and China are all different from one another, even though all are communist. Western and nonaligned nations are even more variable among themselves. Further, each nation has changed from time to time within its own history. To lump all the nations of the world into two categories, or even into three, is probably as distorting as it is helpful in this regard.

The concept of the Third World, increasingly popular in recent years, is a typological disaster, since it also implies that one can generalize broadly about a number of nations which are highly variable in economic, political, cultural, and social terms. Do Canada, Ceylon, and Yugoslavia, for example, really have so much in common, as Irving Louis Horowitz argues, that one can generalize meaningfully about them and draw contrasts to each of the other two worlds?[15] Or, as concerns the major dimensions of culture change, does not Canada have more in common with the United States, in the First World, and Yugoslavia with Hungary or even Russia in the Second? To discuss the earth population in terms of two or three worlds is distorting in many ways. In order to keep our attention on real people facing real problems, then, I propose a more modest effort than surveying all nations would be. I propose to compare just two, India and China.

The comparison of India and China can be particularly informative. In part this is because they align themselves on the two sides of the ideological barrier. But more importantly, each is an enormous country of key importance in international affairs. With large territories and populations of approximately 500 million in India and 700 million in China, they dwarf all other nations. Because they are so large and powerful, whether actually or potentially, they play highly influential roles in world strategies for culture change. Planners all over the world look to them as the two major models for emulation by developing nations. In their success they inspire imitation.

Communication and cultural fit are the two interrelated dimensions we are most concerned with as anthropologists. In the case of India, community development makes good sense in terms of what anthropologists have learned about these factors.

As concerns cultural fit, the Indian approach is to graft innovations onto the solid stem of tradition.[16] It is an approach which emulates the way cultures often evolve when left to themselves. Without interference, it is a slow and gradual process of "changes that represent the accumulation of small variations that, viewed from day to day, are scarcely noticeable."[17] Because droplets of change spend themselves in an ocean of continuity, the process is not disruptive.

The anthropological theory relevant to India, then, is that change takes place successfully when it involves comparatively small additions to an otherwise stable way of life. Given this understanding of process, the problem for planners is to determine how much novelty can be absorbed at any one moment, that is, how much the pace of change can be sped up.

The key to rapid change appears to be successful communication broadly defined. Knowledge of village needs has got to get from villagers to planners. Conversely, planners must succeed in reaching individuals and communities with their programs. For these ends, institutions which can activate and shape communication are prerequisites. In India, the major relevant institution is called the Community Development Program, a body of legislation endorsed by the central government and put into law by each state for itself.[18]

Beginning in 1952 and covering two thirds of India ten years later, the Community Development Program is organized around development blocks of about 100 villages. At this level, under the direction of block development officers, along with experts on agricultural techniques, soil management, animal husbandry, cooperative organizations, medical care, rural industries, and educational methods, needs are assessed, programs organized, and projects supervised. The key individuals, however, are village-level workers, each of whom mediates between the experts and four or five villages in which he lives and works.

It proved more difficult than originally anticipated for peasants to learn about new ideas, accept them, and integrate them into village customs. Communication broke down at various levels, including that of village-level workers. In the latter area, much of the difficulty grew out of the contrast between modern and traditional views of the leadership role.

Traditionally, village leaders have been older, relatively prosperous landowners with strong networks of supporting kinsmen, neighbors, caste mates, and fellow religionists. Village-level workers attempt to carry out a leadership role in the communities for which they are responsible. They instruct in the use of new agricultural equipment, different kinds of seed, improved techniques of animal care, drainage and water supply, medical care, village crafts, and even in ways to make village democracy work. Yet the workers have none of the defining qualifications of leaders. They are different from perhaps all the people they work with in being educated. Often they have acquired some of the sophistication of townsmen. More, they are younger by two or three decades than traditional leaders, they have none of the wealth of prosperous villagers, for they must live on minuscule salaries, and they come into communities where they lack ties to kinsmen and neighbors. Often, as well, they find their caste and religion separate them. It takes great tact and diplomacy to lead with such handicaps.

The key to success sometimes has been to get the support of traditional leaders. The young worker who works through the village headman may find among other villagers a new willingness to listen. The villages, however, are never the quiet, tranquil places they seem to the passing traveler. Typically they are shot through with intrigue and factionalism. Often the response to a proposed innovation is determined by how the worker is regarded as aligned in village rivalries. If he can manage to remain neutral, he may put factionalism to use in his favor. "If a village-level worker reaches even a single leader in each faction, his message is sure to reach all the families of the village."[19]

Village-level workers do not fit the traditional village definition of a leader. Yet they often take on traditional attitudes toward themselves as leaders. In particular, as men of some education, they may share the widespread Indian feeling that manual labor is inappropriate for persons of stature. This inclines them to encourage innovation from a distance, perched on the sidelines, so to speak, in white trousers and shoes. Clearly, to teach and encourage cultivators, the instructor must get into the fields to demonstrate new techniques and equipment.

Perhaps the ultimate role difficulty for village-level workers, however, derives from job training and job definition. Because a large number of trained workers must be produced on rather short notice, most of them are matriculated with about a year of specialized training in village problems. Rarely are they adequately trained in all the techniques they are supposed to teach. Further, much of their time is diverted to bureaucratic tasks of dubious value. Hours which might better be spent in learning more about their work or in helping villagers are devoted instead to keeping records, writing reports, and doing simple clerical tasks which villagers ought to do for themselves.

To the anthropologist, then, the problem of smoothing the path of change is in part a problem of communication in which the status and role of a key figure, the village-level worker, does not fit well with either traditional norms or new needs. When problems are identified, their solutions often suggest themselves. Village-level workers, for example, clearly need more thorough training in the techniques they are to teach. But they also need training in the nature of peasant social organization, attitudes, values, and world view. With this, the workers also need a perspective on their own culture and personalities. Self-image must change. Recruitment and training better calculated to achieve these ends ought to produce a corps of workers equipped for success.

Community development in India faces enormous problems, of which that of the village-level worker is only one. Many are of a kind anthropologists are equipped to diagnose. These include problems in making village democracy work, problems in communication between villages and higher authorities, obstacles to bringing education effectively into the community, hindrances to success in cooperative organizations, blockages in introducing modern medicine to peasants, and many others. As with the challenge of making village-level workers effective, these problems too look solvable in social and cultural terms.

The assumption that these problems are solvable is based on the observation that in certain times and places they have been solved. This is true in pilot studies carried out in India itself. With well-trained, conscientious planners and workers, modern technology was grafted successfully onto village tradition in the Etawah area of Uttar Pradesh in northern India.[20] The result in that case was new prosperity in old villages. A few years sufficed.

In the West, over a period of decades, similar success has been achieved through the same basic process, incremental change. In the United States, many farmers (as distinct from farm laborers) now live much like urban middle class citizens, a dramatic change in which very little of traditional farm culture survives, at least in many areas. Education has been important, but so too have been the agricultural extension agents, who have been highly successful in mediating between the old and the new. More recently, mass communication, including the automobile, closed the gap still remaining between country and town.

In other nations of the West, too, real success is apparent. Denmark, to take a nation I know particularly well, has moved from a disastrous farm situation in the 1870s to relative success in our time.[21] Incremental change, under proper circumstances, can be sped up to bring about major change in a few years. Nearly total change can be accomplished in a decade or two. It is a highly promising strategy for planned change.

In the final analysis, however, cultural and social problems are only part of the difficulty of making development work through incremental change. Ultimately, success or failure depends upon political and economic factors that professional anthropologists are not competent to evaluate. Development requires large financial resources judiciously allocated. India and other nations face extremely grave challenges in these areas. They must have great sums of money, often more than an underindustrialized nation can conjure up, and they must direct that money sagely, without large military budgets, graft, or other misusages. It is on this level, in the end, that success or failure will be determined in countries committed to a policy of incremental change. And it is on this level that India shows the most serious signs of failing.

Ideological differences separating the two worlds of culture change are reflected in action programs which function in contrasting ways. Planned culture change in the communist world generally, and in the People's Republic of China in particular, is not undertaken in a way classifiable as a process of incremental change. Quite the contrary. Community life is reorganized thoroughly and radically in a brief period of time. Does anthropological theory offer any basis for evaluating change of this sort? Clearly it does.

Since 1917, communist governments have attempted to change peasant villages in revolutionary ways. Anthropological theory, however, has taken account of these experiences only tangentially. To some extent, data from communist nations have been incorporated into our thinking on incremental change. But no major revisions of culture change theory have come of it. This is perhaps an understandable product of the secrecy that is imposed. Foreign anthropologists have not been allowed to do field work except in Yugoslavia. What we know of the Soviet Union and mainland China is very incomplete, is to some extent distorted, and is unverifiable by impartial observers. Although the major events of village change can be reconstructed, the way in which data is obtained has scarcely encouraged noncommunist anthropologists to attempt to work with it in their theorizing.

The consequence is that our awareness of an alternative to incremental change was late in coming. When we did learn of it, the source was not a specialist on communist programs but Margaret Mead, who drew upon field work among the Manus, a society of island dwellers just northeast of New Guinea.[22] Manus (Great Admiralty Island) was first investigated by Mead in 1928. At that time, she found herself describing a traditional Melanesian culture. The islanders lived in thatch houses set on stilts over the water. Women shaved their heads, dressed in grass skirts, and wore heavy earrings; men wore bark cloth G-strings and arranged their hair in elaborate ways. Religion focused upon ghosts of the dead, who supervised and judged the conduct of living descendants. Trade and industry were oriented to public displays of dogs' teeth and shell currency. These wealth displays provided occasions for dancing in which men decorated their penes with white ovalis shells and competed in the hard-to-learn technique of what Mead once described as "very rapid leg and body movements which result in the greatest possible gymnastic phallic display."[23] In spite of prolonged contact with colonial powers, in 1928 the Manus still lived very differently from people in the West.

Twenty-five years after her original study, in collaboration with Theodore and Lola R. Schwartz, Margaret Mead undertook a new ethnographic study of the Manus. Where in 1928 she had found "nearly naked savages," in 1953 she found a version of Western culture, a society of practicing Catholics and dedicated democrats who now live in houses built on dry land, wear Western clothing, give tea parties, and are amused or embarrassed to see pictures of themselves and their activities as they once were. The change is radical and thorough, and it took place in about a dozen years, for the precipitating event was World War II.

During the war against Japan, Manus Island became one of the largest American bases in the Pacific. For the first time, the Manus found themselves treated as equals by white men. "The Americans treated us like individuals, like brothers," they recalled later, and rapidly they learned what individuals in the West took for granted as a style of life, whether it was ice cream, modern hospital care, or the all-purpose jeep.[24] Always, the Manus had been dedicated to hard work. Now, suddenly, the goals toward which they worked were transformed. Instead of dogs' teeth, they worked for cash, and instead of the old way of life, they wanted a new way. For a few years, employment with Americans met their new needs for money. Later, they returned to fishing and trading, traditional occupations, except that now profits are used to support a local version of Western life. The change is very pervasive. It took place with great rapidity. Yet it seems not to have caused much discomfort or unhappiness.

In searching out the theoretical implications of her findings, Mead concludes that nearly total, rapid change among the Manus was successful because the whole pattern of life changed. Nothing got out of joint because everything changed at once.[25]

The notion of cultural fit implies that a culture is a functional whole, a system, in which all of its parts—economic activities, technology, family system, religious beliefs, values, and so on—are interrelated and mutually adapted. This is a viewpoint which might be called generic functionalism, and it was introduced into anthropology as part of the theoretical kitbag of Bronislaw Malinowski and A. R. Radcliffe-Brown. Cultures may be more or less well integrated in this sense, but in general, the elements of a culture fit together reasonably well. In contrast to more explicit versions of functional theory, no more than this is implied by the notion of generic functionalism. Changing part of the system—incremental change—is a delicate process because it can disturb the system enough to cause trouble. However, when all parts of the culture are changed at once by exchanging each trait for the corresponding part of a donor culture, then the process can take place relatively free of difficulty. The innovations, though massive in number, are functionally integrated at the moment of borrowing. This sort of change, which we may term systemic change, offers a potentially successful alternative to the process of incremental change.

Explicit in this optimistic evaluation of the potentiality of systemic change is the conclusion that individuals after reaching adulthood are still capable of dramatic changes in their way of life and in their personalities. Generally this has not been noted, for anthropologists commonly have assumed the contrary.[26] Once infants are socialized into the culture of their parents, it has been thought, they resist major change. Yet it is clear that adults can change dramatically. We see it in the farm child in a log cabin who becomes a man of great wealth and power. His culture and personality change enormously. Immigrants to the United States in many instances cease to be Sicilians or Mexicans or Japanese and become thoroughly American, again changing in a radical way.[27]

The great changes of culture which can take place for isolated individuals also can take place for whole communities. Margaret Mead documents this for the Manus. Barbara Gallatin Anderson and I found the same process in a Danish village.[28] Dragor was a parochial maritime community at the turn of the century as we learned of it through elderly informants. In the early decades of the twentieth century, however, it was transformed into a suburb of nearby Copenhagen. The change was rapid, a cultural explosion of the twenties and thirties. From villagers who experienced this change, we learned that it took place with almost no measurable personal, social, or cultural disruption. It was conflict-free in that sense. The reason for the ease of transition, in spite of its relative rapidity and thoroughness, we attribute to the fact that the change was systemic. In this way, a whole community of individuals, much as among the Manus, found it possible to become new people without trauma.

Chinese peasants during the Ch'ing Dynasty were reduced to abject poverty.[29] An insensitive government had permitted land and profits to be appropriated by an elite of landlords, many of whom did not even live any longer in the countryside. The revolution of 1911 got mass support by promising what peasants everywhere ask for. They were told that they would own their own fields and houses. "Land to the Tiller," Sun Yat-sen promised, but it never amounted to anything under the Kuomintang. Chiang Kai-shek, who came to power after the premature death of Sun in 1925, was too dependent upon gentry support to be willing or able to undertake land reform. Not until Mao Tse-tung and his peasant army assumed full control in 1949 did Sun's promise become a reality.[30]

The first years of the Maoist era brought prosperity and optimism to Chinese villages.[31] Sun Yet-sen's land to the tiller program was carried out. It was hard on peasant landlords, who either lost their lives or were reduced to penury. But for the mass of peasants it meant, for the first time in living memory, decent shelter, adequate clothing, nourishing food, and a sense of direction.

In addition to redistribution of the land, other reforms were attempted. Most importantly, in the effort to allocate limited equipment and manpower more effectively, mutual-aid teams were encouraged, often to the point of compulsion on the part of the local party secretary. These teams were composed of six to 20 families that pooled their labor, tools, and farm animals to work the fields of each member family. Many resisted involvement, but some found it a mutually agreeable way to increase productivity.

In all, culture change was successful or at least promising. It was undertaken as a process of incremental change which left the major parts of peasant culture unchanged. The land problem was resolved in terms of traditional tenure understandings. Even mutual-aid teams had some roots in old-fashioned labor exchanges, generally arranged by two families between themselves. In all, it was a policy not greatly different from that of the West.

Rejuvenation of the family farm has no permanent place in Marxist theory. The goal is to pool all resources—labor, equipment, and land—into large collective enterprises. In areas with villages, collectives often take shape as a reorganization of old communities. Ideally, the shift to collectives should take place voluntarily. But while peasants are naturally delighted to own their land, they are equally predictable in showing hostility to the transfer of their land to group ownership. It was hoped in China that experience with mutual-aid teams would incline farmers to want to form agricultural cooperatives. It did not. Up to 1951, only 300 collectives had been formed in all of the nation. By 1953 the number still had reached only 14,000.

Impatient with the slow pace, the regime shifted to mandatory change. According to official figures, between 1955 and 1957, 97 percent of all farming families were forcibly organized into cooperatives. Still dissatisfied, 1958 was turned into the now infamous year of the Great Leap Forward, when the nation's 752,113 collectives were reorganized into 26,000 larger units, the communes. Virtually overnight, hundreds of millions of people were forced to give up their culture for a thoroughly different one.

The change nearly caused the economic and moral collapse of the nation. Yet, as in India, much of the trouble had national rather than local parameters. The political-economic system on that level was not geared to such unprecedented new demands. Drought further complicated the problem. As far as the cultural dimension was concerned, however, the process was one of systemic change, and was therefore not in difficulty simply because it was rapid and pervasive.

Peasant culture change from 1955 on has been an effort to change the whole pattern of peasant life. The end of property ownership eliminated the economic support necessary for joint family, lineage, and clan organization. But in the new order, only the domestic family was permitted to survive, so disfunction was not involved. Contrary to lurid press reports in the West, the domestic family itself was not eliminated. Public mess halls, community nurseries, and schools did not destroy the family. Rather, mothers, their families intact, were pleased that some of their traditional housework could be lightened through use of these new facilities. Senior men no longer dominated families and villages, but their loss of power and prestige coincided with acceptance through a massive indoctrination campaign of a new ethos in which women, the poor, the young, and the uneducated were enfranchised. Religious beliefs were attacked, but Maoism offered a new secular religion for the masses. In all, every aspect of peasant culture changed. The new was a reasonably integrated system. Chinese peasants are as flexible individually as are other populations. Trauma might have been minimal insofar as cultural adjustment was concerned.

Official and otherwise biased reporting suggests success in systemic change. The facts may be different. We cannot be sure that old values, beliefs, and habits have changed as completely as we are told. It is probable that they have not. Certainly, in the Soviet Union, where a comparable strategy of systemic change was set in motion by Stalin in 1928, peasant dissatisfaction with collectivization was evident, and seems related to the survival of peasant forms of family, religious beliefs, work habits, and, above all, values concerning ownership of land, equipment, and the harvest. To make the system work, the government had to acquiesce to an arrangement it finds ideologically disagreeable. Each peasant is allowed to own a small private plot and to use or sell its products as he chooses.

Private plots indicate the problem of culture change in the U.S.S.R. Insofar as they represent the means whereby peasants can adjust to the new demands of collective farming by hanging onto old habits of land usage, private plots represent a strategy of incremental change. Yet they are part of a program of systemic change. In using both strategies, the advantages of either may be lost. The People's Republic of China may well be caught up in the same dilemma.

Collectivization and communalization in China did not take place without human cost. We hear of resistance to change. The velvet glove of persuasion has only thinly disguised the iron fist of force. Here especially it is difficult to evaluate the documentation. The change was resisted. But dictating change included suppression of resistance and punishment for protest. We cannot know the full extent of discouragement and dismay. We can only know that they were there and were substantial. This comes through even in the cheery documentations of Jan Myrdal and William Hinton. It is explicit in the observations of C. K. Yang. It suggests human problems much like those of the U.S.S.R.

One way or the other, underdeveloped nations must accommodate to a new world here and on the horizon. Cultures must change greatly 'for this to be done. Communist and noncommunist strategies on the whole are very different. Insofar as one can evaluate the two in terms of culture change theory, each involves difficulties which greatly discourage those who would take part. At the same time, to the extent that the one favors systemic change and the other incremental change, each strategy looks possible as a program in applied anthropology. As concerns developing nations, it is not clear that we will avoid wandering in the wilderness, but one still dares to hope we will someday reach the Promised Land.

# 7        Armageddon

Pick up a newspaper and you encounter a range of problems—not just "little" problems, but immense, explosive, dangerous problems that seem to threaten the very survival of civilization and even of human life. You read of war, war crimes, genocide, racism, mass violence, urban decline, moral turpitude—in all, a Pandora's Box of ecological, populational, ethical, and technological threats. When I pick up my morning paper I often think of what Max Weber answered when asked the purpose of his sociological research. "I want to see how much I can stand."[1] At any moment, World War III, the final battle of Armageddon, could easily become a reality.

Whether important and powerful persons or merely concerned citizens and thoughtful individuals, we obviously need guidelines for analyzing problems and proposing solutions. Such guidelines must be based upon some kind of fundamental view of the world, some kind of political philosophy or social theory. For some people, this is carefully thought out and consciously expressed. For many, it is merely unconsciously assumed and naively accepted.

The sociologist C. Wright Mills has described this need for social theory as the need to know "where we stand and where we are going."[2] In other words, we need to know what we want and how we can get it, not only in terms of a specific problem, but more basically in terms of the kind of world we want and how we might work to create such a world.

We face great urgency in our time to know what we want and how we can get it, because the world has become something that man has never known before. With a rapidity that astounds the layman and overwhelms the historian, we find ourselves suddenly living in a world of virtually instantaneous global intercommunication. An astronaut can circle the globe in 90 minutes. An ordinary traveler can cross an ocean in hours. A missile can traverse a continent in minutes. Verbal communication across the world takes place in microseconds.

Living in a world of instantaneous communication where action and reaction, stimulus and response, can take place in seconds and minutes, we find a world divided in two as concerns where we stand and where we are going. On the one side we find the communist camp that defines the goals it wants and the steps it must take to reach them in terms of the social theory of Karl Marx, his collaborators, and his successors. On the other side we find noncommunists who seek different goals and use different methods for social change.

Within each camp is considerable disagreement over what we should aim for and what we should do. It is no easy matter to generalize about either camp. Yet the need to understand the issues involved is urgent; for modern science and technology have created not only a world of instantaneous interaction, but also a capacity for unlimited destruction, not only of one camp by the other, but of human society as a whole. Under such circumstances, we would be very foolish if we did not carefully examine "where we stand and where we are going," however difficult the task. And this means a careful, objective examination not only of ideas about society that underlie policy in the West, in our own camp, but also those of the other camp, those originating in the work of Karl Marx.

To enunciate a social theory is difficult. For one thing, it is difficult as an intellectual exercise because the problems involved are extremely complex. The number of variables important in any social event is enormous. They include social, cultural, psychological, biological, and physical dimensions, and each dimension is itself a complex thing. Further, we cannot ordinarily study such events in a laboratory situation, where most variables can be held constant while those under study are examined. Yet, for all its complexity, and despite unique characteristics that distinguish it from sciences such as physics and biology, social theory is like chemical, biological, mathematical, and other theories in that it is a systematic, rational search for answers about the world we live in.

In a sense, however, social theory involves a difficulty which greatly complicates the work of the theorist and which is not usually a problem for scholars in other disciplines. Because social theory may find expression in the actual design and function of society, because it may have an impact upon the daily activities of individuals, in short, because the working out of social theory may to some degree determine the quality of the society in which you and I live, including the very life chances of each of us, social theorizing carries a heavy emotional load. It involves personal commitment. It implies a personal bias.

The emotional element in social theorizing cannot be eliminated. To a degree it is even useful and desirable. But to the extent that it represents a bias—a tendency to distort perception and judgment—to that extent it is an ever present danger in the quest for answers.

This caution against emotional bias, always appropriate, is especially necessary when we deal with Karl Marx. Our basic attitudes and opinions are formed in early years when critical judgment is immature. Many of our specific opinions derive from newspapers, magazines, political or religious oratory, and other sources whose coin of persuasion is often pure emotion and whose intent is frequently propagandistic. We must therefore be especially alert to the danger of bias. Many Americans assume that Karl Marx was some sort of monster. This judgment is wrong. "One cannot do justice to Marx without recognizing his sincerity," writes a hostile critic of the man. "His open-mindedness, his sense of facts, his distrust of verbiage, and especially of moralizing verbiage, made him one of the world's most influential fighters against hypocrisy and Pharisaism."[3]

Marx was not a monster. Neither is Marxism as a social theory diabolical in intent. At the level of basic ideals, Marxism is humanistic and well intentioned. As C. Wright Mills has observed, Marx wanted a world in which all men would live well.[4] To this end, he insisted on the importance of rationalism, freedom, and individualism. The ideals of Marx are not fundamentally different from those that underlie the American way of life and the American political system.

The theoretical disagreements that separate the world today into two hostile camps are not on the level of ultimate ideals. They are about the kind of sociey that can best support these ideals of well-being for all men. It is on the level of how such a society can best be formed from the kind of society we have inherited. On this level there certainly is serious disagreement. It is on this level that we must examine Marx in an unbiased, rational way.

Marxism is often treated as a kind of secular religion. The historian Lynn White, Jr., has said that "Marxism, like Islam, is a Judeo-Christian heresy."[5] The nature of Marx's social theory lends itself, in a way that most social theories do not, to being accepted and believed in as a body of immutable truth. This is because one of Marx's basic premises was determinism. His approach to the prediction and control of social change assumes that the course of history is preordained, that the general trends of history have been determined by recognizable causes, and that the social analyst has only to see these causes clearly in order to predict the broad tendencies of the future. Through an analysis of trends in the past, one can extrapolate into the future and know the shape of things to come.

I am not speaking here of predictions which apply to limited places, circumscribed events, and short periods of time. Predictions of this sort are made every day in the social sciences. Applied anthropologists rely on their ability to make limited predictions or probability statements every time they cope with problems such as how to get Venezuelan peasant mothers to give powdered milk to their babies or Alaskan Eskimo to shift from sea hunting to reindeer herding.

Marx's efforts to foresee the future went far beyond predictions of this sort. In fact, they are better termed prophecies than predictions.[6] By his methods, Marx felt that he could prophesy the future state of society as a whole. The most fundamental doctrine in Marxism is that historical prediction (prophecy) is the scientific way of approaching social problems.

This doctrine has two essential features. First, it assumes that society progresses in response to certain immutable forces, above all in response to economic forces. In broad outline, the course of development is inevitable. The nature of society in the year 2000 was inherent (immanent) in the earliest culture of villagers. The society we know live in and the society we can look forward to were and are predetermined.

The second feature of this doctrine is that it has implications for planners. For the determinist, the job of social analysis is to study known societies in order to determine the nature of this preordained society. Once this is known—and Marxists are confident they know it—the later and ultimate stages of social progress can be predicted. The analyst can then use this knowledge to facilitate the changes that will occur. He can hurry them up and make transitions smoother. In the words of Marx, he can hope "to shorten and lessen the birth pangs" of the coming epoch.[7]

Marxist doctrine builds upon the assumptions that the course of history is inevitable (the possibility of prophecy) and that the future can be influenced by knowing this (the use of prophecy). You can see the appeal of such an approach. If it is true that history is preordained, and if it is true that Marxists have the key to this future, then concerned citizens and political activists can work with conviction and self-confidence. As with the devout of a religion which prophesies the future and offers a path to salvation, a political theory such as Marxism can so grip people that they regard dissent as sinful and revision as heresy.

Social theory concerns many kinds of scholars. Each kind has his own basis for examination and evaluation, and anthropology is no exception. One way in which anthropologists can look at Marxism is in terms of what they have learned about cultural evolution. Predictions made by Marx in the nineteenth century as well as others made within the last few years can be examined and evaluated in terms of evolutionary theory.

Marshall D. Sahlins contributed importantly to contemporary evolutionary theory in 1960 when he drew attention to the distinction which can be made between specific and general evolution.[8] Whether in biological or in cultural evolution, he argued, two distinguishable yet inseparable processes may take place as organisms or traditions change; the one is specific, the other, general.

Specific evolution concerns a given entity as it changes and adapts to the environment in which it is located. This is evolution as it leads to diversity. We see specific evolution in the biological world as each kind of animal makes its own unique adaptation. Among monkeys, to illustrate, langurs and colobus species are the products of specializations which allow them to live on coarse leaves where other tree-dwelling monkeys must have more tender fare. Baboons and macaques, for their part, have developed physical and behavioral traits so that they can move away from trees to feed on terrestrial food resources (but where they also face the danger of predators). Within each species, further ramifications are observable. The end product is an impressive diversity of species, subspecies, and varieties, each adapted to its own ecological niche.

Cultures also diversify in the process of specific evolution. Local adaptation and isolation have resulted in great heterogeneity of customs as each society stays alive and gives meaning to life in terms of its own environment. Forest hunters, plains cultivators, grassland herders, coastal fishermen, and many others are all different, and within each category still further differences are apparent. Tibetan herders, Kazakhs, Yokuts, Lapps, Vlachs, the Nuer, and many others are all herders, but they are also all diverse in significant ways. Ultimately, each represents a unique culture adapted to unique circumstances.

Specific evolution is a process about which we can generalize in only a limited sense. Julian H. Steward especially has drawn our attention to the sort of regularities one can best identify on this level.[9] Given a kind of technology—for example, that of hunting peoples who have no mode of locomotion other than their feet and no weapons more effective than the bow and arrow or the spear—and given a kind of environment—say, scrub land and desert—you get regularities in core culture (basic culture) in various places throughout the world where these ecological (technological and environmental) factors are comparable—in this case, underlying similarities such as band organization and patriliny that characterize such widely spread and mutually isolated peoples as the Bushmen in South Africa, the Semang of Malaysia, the Australian aborigines, and a number of others.[10] Such cultural-ecological recurrences are limited. Steward refers to them as the products of what he terms multilinear evolution, thus suggesting that different combinations of environment with technology give different cultural-ecological cores. Certainly, insofar as specific evolution is a universal process, the result has been diversity rather than uniformity, so one cannot predict from the experience of one society the end product—emergent cultures as wholes or as systems—for all societies.

General evolution constitutes a different kind of statement about long-term biological or cultural change. From this perspective, unique products and multilinear differences are disregarded. The view is of change as a succession of types which, however different in other ways, represent increasingly high levels of progress, whether one measures in terms of structural organization (simple to complex) or capacity to capture energy (increasing amounts of energy harnessed). Primate grades and levels of sociocultural integration from band to modern civilization represent evolutionary stages in this sense.

From amoeba to man, general evolution can be documented as a statement about organic development in which greater complexity and increasing energy capture succeed lesser. As concerns culture, Leslie White is the anthropologist who first drew attention to culture as "an elaborate thermodynamic, mechanical system" in a similar sense.[11] Measuring evolutionary progress in terms of "the amount of energy harnessed per capita per year" together with "the efficiency of the instrumental means of putting the energy to work," White summarized world history as a "unilineal" (general evolutionary) sequence of four cultural types. The earliest consisted of social systems based upon human energy (hunting and gathering peoples). Later, people learned to depend upon animal power (agricultural and pastoral cultures). More recently, a fuel age appeared in which man put coal, oil, and natural gas to use. In our time, the use of atomic power seems to mark the beginning of the highest stage yet of general cultural (unilinear, that is, straight-line, progressive) evolution.[12]

Marshall Sahlins summarizes the two different kinds of processes by noting that "specific evolution is 'descent with modification,' " the adaptive radiation of life which gives variety to earth forms. General evolution, on the other hand, "is the progressive emergence of higher life 'stage by stage.' " Adaptation in specific evolution is progressive only in the sense that the organism or culture shifts "from less to more adjusted to a given habitat." The product is either unique or limited in the extent to which it is replicated (shows multilinear regularities). In contrast, progress in general evolution "is passage from less to greater energy exploitation, lower to higher levels of integration, and less to greater all-round adaptability." Only from the perspective of general evolution (unilinear evolution) do you get the arrangement of forms into a sequence of "stages of over-all development" which have meaning for the total universe of organic or cultural forms.[13]

Karl Marx was a nineteenth century pioneer in the development of evolutionary theory. He was unquestionably the most sophisticated theoretician of his time in that regard. He worked in terms of epochs, each defined by its structural form. From (1) a hypothetical (and, we now know, nonexistent) primitive communism, the sequence of epochs was (2) ancient (slave), (3) feudal, (4) capitalist, and, at that time entirely in the future and thus hypothetical, (5) socialist.[14]

It is important to realize that these Marxist stages, insofar as they are not merely hypothetical, are the more or less unique products of specific evolution. They do not constitute successive stages in the process of general evolution. This is particularly clear as regards the feudal epoch. In terms of energy and complexity, feudalism is not a higher stage than ancient society, but a lower one.[15] It represents a decline in the use of energy as the per capita access to animal power fell off. It represents devolution in complexity as social, political, and economic organization fell from the achievements of Rome to parochialism in the Middle Ages, a time when the "political and economic fabric disintegrate[d]."[16]

Feudalism is nearly unique as a phenomenon of specific evolution. It is not a stage of general evolution. The historian Rushton Coulborn found only one close parallel, that of pre-Meiji Japan, plus possible parallels in Chou China, Mesopotamia, Egypt, and India, but no more.[17] Similarly for the other epochs; each that has actually existed appears to represent at most the limited recurrences of multilinear evolution rather than universal, unilineal stages. That being so, one cannot predict that one epoch necessarily will evolve to the next higher insofar as progress may take place.

This challenge to the predictive capacity of Marxism becomes clearer as we examine it more closely. The great achievement of Marx was to compel social scientists to recognize economic forces as prime movers in social change. Anthropologists have found no reason to reject this as a broad, generic statement about general evolution. Leslie White's model for cultural organization exemplifies both the impact of Marxism in this generic sense—what Robert H. Lowie referred to as "giving proper weight to the material basis of society"—and the explanatory potential it has as part of the perspective of general evolution.[18]

A culture, in White's view, consists of three interrelated subsystems: technological, sociological, and ideological.[19] Technological development shapes evolution in the other two. "The technological system is basic and primary," writes White. "Social systems are functions of technologies; and philosophies express technological forces and reflect social systems." This leads White to conclude, "The technological factor is therefore *the* determinant of a cultural system as a whole."[20]

Implicit in the Marxist dialectic is the notion that economic changes occur prior to, and are determinants of, associated sociocultural development. Marx and Engels spelled out this view in conceptualizing the superstructure of the social system as shaped by an economic substructure of which the chief element consists of rather vaguely defined forces of production. Marxist predictions seem to find general support in White's theorizing, but the appearance is deceptive. In part, it is deceptive because White's formulation has meaning only as a statement about general evolution; the Marxian scheme is a statement about specific evolution. It is also deceptive because it confuses abstractions with realities.

The stages of general evolution are highly abstract. Though based upon a knowledge of real societies, they are not real societies in themselves, but glosses on real societies. Thus, to say that material change necessarily comes before social and ideological change is meaningful only as a shorthand statement about history in terms of first occurrences. Each stage may have appeared as one society first experienced technological or economic change and then witnessed compensatory changes in other aspects of social life. But from this you cannot predict the way in which specific societies will develop, because real societies coexist with one another in various stages of development, and through cultural borrowing (acculturation), the sequence of development can be turned topsy-turvy.

A society may evolve, as Marx and White have argued, in a sequence which subordinates sociological and ideological advances to technological or economic change. But a society may also evolve through adaptation to other societies by means of acculturation. In such cases, it often happens that the social system or idea system changes in advance of significant economic change. In many underdeveloped areas, for example, the first impetus to change clearly has been ideological. Many nations began to modernize as increasing contact with the outside world brought them new aspirations and understandings. Only later were many of these nations consolidated politically, and it was later still, if at all, that the economic system was able fully to support a new view of the world and a modern organization of society. This reverses the order of technology, social organization, and ideology. Yet we see it in many places, including India and mainland China, where ideologies first influenced man to hope for change, after a time resulted in political reorganization, and only later, and in our day still with incomplete success, led to economic revolution.

The point is that Marx did a brilliant job of analyzing forces of change within the specific societies which constituted prototypes for his ancient, feudal, and capitalist epochs. But he failed to provide a basis for predicting future developments either in other real societies or as general stages of evolution. His efforts to predict can be attacked on various grounds, and I am mentioning only a few criticisms which are particularly grounded in anthropology. Ultimately, however, perhaps the most convincing way to demolish the belief in scientific predictions is to point out simply that many of the predictions of Marx and Engles did not come true.

A century and more has passed since Marx wrote, a long period of time during which capitalism as he knew it has changed to something quite different from what it once was. On the whole, the transformation of capitalist society in Western Europe and the United States has not taken place as predicted. Much that Marx and Engels said would happen has not occurred. Importantly, the middle class did not disappear through a polarization of the class system into a small class of very rich exploiters and a gigantic mass of cruelly exploited workers. Instead, the middle class has grown increasingly wealthier and more powerful. Nor did the working class decline more and more into misery.

In the United States and Western Europe we have witnessed increases in wages, not decreases. We have witnessed decreases in hours of work, not increases. We have witnessed an end to child labor, not its exacerbation. In the same fashion, we have seen female labor evolve in a direction which gives the hope of opportunities for creative achievement and professional advancement equal to those that man enjoy. And instead of seeing increased misery, we have witnessed the emergence of a society in which the major part of the population is coping with the problem of affluence, a situation in which the majority must face the problem of finding meaning in life beyond the mere possession of ample leisure and material possessions and in which we are now working to eliminate poverty and misery in minority populations and among the "hidden" poor. I do not for an instant minimize the gravity of persistent problems, but for evaluating Marx it needs to be stressed that he anticipated a level of gross exploitation of the majority of the population which has not materialized. Further, since on both theoretical and pragmatic grounds the Marxist capacity to predict must be abandoned, we clearly must abandon the prediction that the future of world society inevitably is socialist in the Marxian definition.

It is scarcely surprising that a nineteenth century theory should need revising. The study of Marx is merely the starting point for understanding Marxism in our time. Modern socialist and communist theoreticians do not insist on the rightness of Marx without admitting changes which range from mere additions or elaborations to extensive revisions and corrections.[21]

One of the most persuasive of later theoretical trends has grown out of a major failure in Marx's efforts to predict. Marx was convinced that the communist revolution would first take place in France, Germany, the United States, or some other industrial nation. In such a nation he expected a revolutionary force to take shape as the working class led in revolt. Yet communist revolutions did not explode in industrial or industrializing nations in this way. Instead, they occurred in preindustrial, agrarian nations. Communist successes in Russia, Yugoslavia, China, Cuba, and elsewhere were quite unexpected. They built upon peasant instead of working class insurrection. Marx was convinced that peasants did not have what it takes to rebel. It took Lenin, Tito, Mao, and Castro with their peasant armies to prove how wrong he could be.

Leon Trotsky, looking back at the success of the Bolshevik Revolution, concluded that it was possible because of what he termed "the privilege of historic backwardness." Precisely because she was backward, Russia in 1917 was able to modernize efficiently. She could skip the whole series of intermediate stages which capitalist nations had struggled through for 150 years, and which they were still saddled with to some extent. "Arising late," he wrote, "Russian industry did not repeat the development of the advanced countries, but inserted itself into this development, adapting their latest achievements to its own backwardness."[22]

Although Mao Tse-tung is scarcely a Trotskyite, he apparently finds the doctrine of the privilege of historic backwardness congenial, for he has written: "Apart from other characteristics, our people . . . [are] characterized by poverty and by vacuity which is like that of a sheet of blank paper. This may seem to be a bad thing, whereas in reality it is a good one." He goes on, "Nothing is written on a sheet of paper which is still blank, but it lends itself admirably to receive the latest and most beautiful words and the latest and most beautiful pictures."[23]

The anthropologist Elman R. Service has reformulated this concept of the advantage of primitiveness into what he calls the law of evolutionary potential.[24] Basing his analysis upon Sahlin's distinction of two kinds of evolutionary process, Service draws attention to specific evolution as a process of adaptation in which success requires specialization.

It has been noted that in biological evolution, general evolutionary advance does not occur in highly specialized species, but rather in those with a broader, more flexible relationship to their environment. "[T]here is no certain case on record of a line showing a high degree of specialization giving rise to a new type," observed Julian Huxley in 1943. "All new types which themselves are capable of adaptive radiation seem to have been produced by relatively unspecialized ancestral lines."[25]

Assuming that what is true for biological evolution applies as well to cultural—and this is where he errs—Service explains his law of evolutionary potential as follows: "The more specialized and adapted a form in a given evolutionary stage, the smaller is its potential for passing to the next stage." Or, put differently, "Specific evolutionary progress is inversely related to general evolutionary potential."[26] In other words, the very achievement of a modern nation militates against its future revolutionary success, for success brings with it the evolutionary barrier of specialization. Conversely, a backward nation, not yet specialized, has the capacity to leapfrog more advanced countries as world culture moves to the next higher stage of evolution, that of a socialist world.

In the grand sweep of history, one appears to find confirmation of the law of evolutionary potential. Rome, a backwater of Greece, took up and developed ancient society. The United States, at first a primitive outpost of European civilization, in recent times has been the pacesetter for the world. Russia, very backward in comparison with Western Europe, now is equally a world leader. Japan, a primitive attachment to China in past centuries, in the twentieth joined the top rank of modern, industrial powers. On first appraisal, at least, an understanding of this law appears to put one in a position to make highly provocative predictions for modern societies.

Professor Service makes two predictions which particularly require our attention. First, one must conclude, he argues, and Mao Tse-tung agrees, that the dominant power in the near future will likely be that behemoth of the Far East, China, because at this moment in history, China has the advantage of backwardness. Second, the United States must fall from its current high position to be overtaken by retarded nations. Further, since the advantage of prediction is to be able "to shorten and lessen the birth pangs" of the coming epoch, Service has constructive suggestions about how best to plan for this future which evolutionary law reveals as inevitable.

America must soon give up its privileges as the world's most powerful nation, the argument goes. This is inevitable. It would be wise for us to recognize this inevitability, to cooperate fully with developing nations, to provide them with development capital totally free of conditions and restraints, to assist them in every way. By behaving in this manner, we would reduce tensions and minimize residual hostility toward the American people. We could hope, then, to be permitted to survive as a nation, much as Greece survived when Rome became powerful.

Under Rome, Greece was shorn of power and reduced in wealth. She was not hated or despised, however. On the contrary, her old reputation as the seedbed of civilization made it possible for her to survive under the Romans as a highly esteemed center of learning. Greece lived on as the best place for higher education, attracting young aristocrats from all over the Empire. Greeks were admired somewhat as are very old genteel but now poor Boston families when they come to the attention of Texas oil magnates. By catering to the wishes of the leaders of backward nations, Service appears to say, the United States may hope to survive the world revolution intact, reduced in circumstances, but respected like a dowager queen in the ruins of her past.

I do not object entirely to Service's prescription for civilizational health. I can easily agree that it is essential to the future well-being of the United States that the rest of the world be successful in efforts to modernize. But I do object to the notion that governmental decisions can be guided by scientific predictions, and specifically that the law of evolutionary potential is a useful guide. Insofar as that law implies more than a simple recurrence in history of great nations falling and new ones rising, the law is pure nonsense.

From an economist's point of view, Abba Lerner has demolished this argument in a sentence. He and I were team-teaching a course on the social sciences in Berkeley a couple of years ago when I introduced this evolutionary law for discussion. "If that law were valid," Dr. Lerner pointed out, "then the smartest thing the United States could do to assure industrial success would be to destroy all of its industry in order to have the advantage of starting from nothing." Of course that would be preposterous. But so, too, is the belief that you can plan by large-scale predicting.

The law of evolutionary potential is not a basis for making scientific predictions in the grand manner because it does not describe an inevitable process. One country may leapfrog another, as history has shown. But most nations which have been backward in the past remain backward. Further, great nations may decline and fall. But they may also persist for centuries. They may even reconstitute themselves in a revolutionary way.

Rome disappeared as a power and as a center of civilization—but not in the first century B.C., when the republic displayed alarming symptoms of collapse. At that time, some backwater kingdom, I suppose, might expectably have surpassed it if there were an advantage to backwardness. Instead, Rome reconstructed itself as an empire, and went on for three centuries and more to heights undreamed of earlier. And if Rome provides a pattern for good treatment of a dethroned civilization, why not also for a nation that might reconstitute itself for future centuries of success? History gives precedent for either course, not merely for the one. The law of evolutionary potential describes a possible but not an inevitable process. It is therefore not a law at all. It is not even a statement of probability. At most it says what is possible.

History is not predetermined; the future is not preordained. An anthropological perspective offers no basis for believing that planning can be done in terms of reliable predictions concerning the wider dimensions of future social and political institutions. We can speak of possibilities. We can even speculate about probabilities. But we cannot know about certainties, because the future is still up for grabs.

An anthropological perspective cannot predict world civilization for the twenty-first century. But it can say something about how such a civilization can be built. It can put the social structure in human perspective, for it gives full force to the power of individuals and ideas to shape the future.

The perspective is still that of cultural evolution. The theorist is Margaret Mead.[27] The conclusion is that individuals of genius, the interpreters and shapers of their cultures, can give direction to the course of human events if they have power or influence and if they are joined with stimulating collaborators. "The effectiveness of a genius appears to be highly dependent not only on the state of the culture and the period in which such an individual is born," Mead observes, "but also on the exact position in the social structure which he occupies and the exact composition of the cooperative face-to-face group within which he acts."[28]

The key to the future, in other words, is the capacity each society has to place gifted individuals in small, stimulating groups with power. Whether for villages, nations, or world governments, the social or political structure must allow thinking individuals effectively to shape the direction of change. The direction chosen, of course, will depend upon the values cherished. The cultural background of leaders is most significant in this regard. Jesus and his disciples turned much of mankind in a direction potentially supportive of brotherhood. Adolf Hitler and his ministers also shaped human destiny, but their ideal was racist and megalomanic. The promise of evolutionary theory, in short, is not an inalterable destiny. In fact, it is not really a promise, but a chance. And it is not a map to the future, but the tool for making maps. Civilizations have been built this way before. That precedent is our only promise. The opposition of communist and anticommunist is really a challenge as to which is better able to place brilliant but thoughtful men in positions which give power, but which also give free rein to reason and high ideals. If both kinds of governments were to succeed in this way, we all would be the winners.

The hope of the future depends upon the success governments will have in providing rational leadership. One can easily become pessimistic over this. Certainly, communist nations do not inspire confidence. The talk one hears of people's democracies is pure rhetoric. Communist governments, like many that are reactionary, are dictatorships. The men in power have gotten there by gaining a monopoly on control of force. Further, they remain in power by maintaining totalitarian control. And this is the great shortcoming of dictatorships.

Totalitarian governments have some real advantages in modernization. Often they are uniquely able to get things done. The leaders can make decisions without dispute and implement them without delay. Adolf Hitler built freeways where no previous government had been able to get the necessary land rights, planning agreements, and financing. Benito Mussolini made the trains run on time, and in the Italy of his day, that was an extraordinary achievement.

Totalitarian governments can get things done. And when their decisions are rational, they can achieve great things. The fatal flaw is that rationality cannot be assured. There is no guarantee that the men in control will be the geniuses Margaret Mead was talking about. Their only genius may be to get power. Adolf Hitler got the depression-plagued industry of Germany on its feet, but his genius was tinged with madness, and when he was finished he had led his nation and much of the world to disaster. Mussolini enjoyed early success in Italy, but in the end his judgment proved bad. He also led his nation to disaster.

In some nations, the consequences of dictatorship have not been so obviously tragic. In Spain, General Franco can say with pride that he has given his nation peace for over three decades. And like Hitler and Mussolini, he too can point to some improvements. He built a new university in Madrid, for one thing. Yet look again at that university. The buildings are modern and impressive, but science, scholarship, art, and literature for the most part have languished. The regime has also built new highways, but they run through villages that are impoverished. "Of all the countries in which I have traveled, only India and Turkey have had rural poverty as grinding as that in Spain," writes James A. Michener, "and the much publicized 'Twenty-five Years of Peace' have brought little to the farmers."[29] Since farmers and villagers comprise about three fourths of the total population, grinding poverty is nearly a universal fact of life on the Iberian Peninsula.

Even benevolent dictators may have poor judgment. Further, the very circumstances of maintaining a dictatorship tend to increase the chances for leadership to be irrational. To stay in power, fascist leaders usually forbid open criticism of the government. Newspapers, radio, and television are strictly censored. Novelists and painters are kept under control. Scientists are supervised. Public forums are forbidden. Only that which is acceptable to the regime is allowed expression. All dissent, all honest criticism, all unwanted information, is suppressed. The result of suppression is not merely that the populace lives in ignorance, bad as that is. The result is that the leadership itself comes increasingly to live in isolation from the people they rule and the world they live in. Rational decisions cannot be made when the facts dealt with are hidden and distorted.

Because dictatorships suppress freedom of expression, they always are in danger of functioning irrationally. The censorship of mass media, the punishment of dissenting intellectuals, and the proscription of public meetings are characteristic of dictatorships. We recognize these symptoms in Nazi Germany and fascist Italy. They have been characteristic of Spain. But they also are fully present in every nation that flies the red flag of communism. It is this suppression, and the irrationality that it represents, which most discourages optimism about the communist solution.

Dictatorship is a deceit. It seems to promise efficiency and action, but in fact it can lead to catastrophe. The alternative, therefore, has to be some form of democracy.

During World War II and for some years after, we in the West were convinced that the main thing necessary to assure the success of developing nations was to see to it that they got some form of democratic government. That hope, too, was a deceit, at least in part. Democracy has not worked well where we thought it was bound to succeed. In many places, it was transformed almost immediately into dictatorship. In 1961, "high-life" bands in Accra were singing "Ghana is free now," but by the fall of 1962, President Kwame Nkrumah had established totalitarian control.

In other nations, democracy persists, but an inability to take action makes one question the likelihood of long-term viability. India, in particular, exemplifies the dimmed hopes of many of us. Where every region and faction has a voice in government, it can be nearly impossible to get consensus on any governmental program. India seems in imminent danger of falling apart from internal disputes.

To investigate these problems of national integration, one needs the special skills of a political scientist. But in countries such as India, democracy involves problems on the local as well as the national and international levels, and local problems especially fall within the competence of anthropologists. It is said, for example, that peasant villages offer a good potential base for the building of democracy because villages are very egalitarian, with an opportunity for each individual to experience direct participation in the political process.[30] In fact, as many anthropologists can report, peasant villages in general, and Indian villages in particular, tend to remain under the control of local elites, even when they have the form of elected governments. If anything, village political life prepares peasants to accede to authoritarian leadership rather than to participate in democratic government.

Ignorance and parochialism among the masses present still another kind of threat to effective democracy. Many inexperienced voters in the first national elections in India seemed quite uncertain of what they were doing. It is hard to credit them with an understanding of the issues they were deciding. The journalist Kusum Nair reports talking with one villager who admitted to hearing of the Congress Party and discussing it, but then added, apparently as an afterthought, "now that you mention it, we do not know whether Congress is a man or a woman."[31]

Where the masses are brought up to acquiesce to minority control, where illiteracy and isolation leave people unable to understand complex issues, and where every region and faction remains loyal primarily to its own special interests, democracy will be in serious trouble. In many nations today, these conditions prevail, and democracy is indeed not working well.

The search for rationality in government, then, leads to a dilemma. For developing nations, dictatorship is a deceit but democracy is a cripple. Whether or not we can find our way out of that dilemma will determine whether our future is to be a millennium of peace and prosperity or the Armageddon of an atomic holocaust.

Anthropology offers a perspective on man, though the nature of that perspective depends a great deal on who the anthropologist is. In my view, certain major themes are prominent.

The question of where the Garden of Eden might have been draws attention to the comparative recency of man's ascent from lower animals. Some writers are so impressed with the closeness of man to his animal origins that they see warfare and the threat of self-annihilation as primarily a product of surviving instincts. I do not agree. The instincts of man are greatly modified by human culture, and purely biological explanations for complex forms of human behavior must be dismissed as simplistic and distortive.

Yet the closeness of man to lower animals is a fact, which does mean that we have no greater claim to immortality than they do. Dinosaurs ruled the earth for millions of years, and during those years they had the appearance of permanence. Now they are extinct. To most men, it is inconceivable that we could become as extinct as Tyrannosaurus or the mastodon. Clearly we could. It is a sobering lesson.

In looking for the first Adam, we saw the humanity of man as a number of qualities which slowly developed over a long period of time. This is cause for hope, not for despair. Man is not a creature suddenly created and forever the same. If he was upright long before he had language, and if he could speak long before he was an artist, then he can develop still more. Perhaps after being like us for so long a time, he someday may evolve new capabilities to make him even more distinctive as a human being, and the process selects for improvements.

That man may evolve into something even more distinctively human is a viewpoint quite foreign to most men. Without doubt we might develop organically in ways which could make us as we are now seem as primitive to future men as Java man seems to us. Yet the evolution of man seems increasingly to have taken cultural rather than organic forms, and it is in culture change that we primarily look for modification and improvement.

The grip of culture on the nature of man is undoubtedly the single most important lesson one learns from anthropology. In looking at language we come most directly to grips with this reality. Language is a product of cultural development, yet the very view one has of oneself, the very way in which one perceives the world and thinks about it, appears to reside in the language one speaks and thus ultimately in the culture one has inherited. Personality is shaped by culture, even as culture responds to human personality. This close linkage of individual and cultural identity makes it meaningful to contrast man to the lower animals and to see him as endowed with special qualities and unusual capabilities. The archeological record provides a basis for humility, but it provides a basis for human self-confidence as well.

Although the search for Adam leads one to recognize the importance of cultural factors in human development, it leads one also to see man as still an animal in some ways. This is most important to realize insofar as it makes us aware that the bodies we possess developed as organisms specialized for hunting. Only in recent millennia have we evolved beyond our Mesolithic ancestors. We still possess bodies intended for the active life of a hunter, yet many of us spend our days sitting at desks or standing behind counters in largely sedentary occupations. Medical findings confirm what the fossil record suggests: for good health, we need to find substitutes for the running, deep breathing, and body fatigue we so recently have given up. In other ways, too, we must never forget that the potentialities of culture change are circumscribed. Always they must take account of the limitations and possibilities of human anatomy.

The mark of Cain symbolizes a nearly unique quality of the human condition, one that has brought endless pain and heartache. Men kill other men, and warfare is an ancient part of the human heritage. Knowing something of its early history, however, offers a basis for hope. Man has not always been a warrior. Undoubtedly he always has fought to defend himself against aggressors, and at times early hominids must have been aggressors. But not until some 10,000 years ago did warfare become a central feature of tribal cultures and a dominant shaper of human personalities.

Knowing something of how warfare emerged suggests something of how it can be subdued. Human greed seems to have encouraged warfare, and that suggests the needs for new economic and political structures to allow the poor access to the good things in life without the temptation to use force. It also suggests the need for new attitudes toward wealth. Population crowding seems to have encouraged warfare, and unquestionably the effective control of population growth is essential if we are to have peace. Finally, both warfare and peace require the mobilization of social forces, which suggests that ultimate success in the quest for peace will require success in the creation of social and political structures capable of organizing men for it. These are not answers to the problems of war and peace, of course, but they do indicate where at least some of the answers may be found.

In reminding ourselves of Noah's curse, we remind ourselves of yet another feature of man's lot. Man has learned to domesticate not only lower animals, but other men as well. The inequities of peasant, slave, and minority status are the consequence. Anthropologists have much to say about these inequities, but the single most important contribution probably is what we can say about race. We find that human populations do differ in their biological heredity. But they do not differ in all organic qualities. Natural selection appears to have resulted in worldwide uniformities in those hominid traits which under any circumstances provide an advantage to men. And the single most important of these universals is general intelligence. All races appear to be equal in mental ability.

In questions of race, as in human behavior generally, an understanding of the interdependence of culture and personality is essential. Individuals from deprived minorities, whether racially distinctive or not, often perform significantly lower on intelligence tests. The reason for poor performance does not appear to lie in heredity. As we have seen, all larger populations appear equally endowed with general intelligence. Rather, the reason seems to lie in the effect of social discrimination on personality, including such psychological aptitudes as self-confidence and high motivation, but also such basic qualities as general knowledge and language skills. The effects of racial or other discrimination reach into the individual psyche. This is an important part of the perspective of anthropology.

In our time we look for the Promised Land in terms of many different ideologies. Almost all of us, though, include the raising of living standards for deprived peoples as an essential part of our view of what the good life ought to be. As anthropologists, we still are looking for the theoretical tools we need in order to contribute to this goal more fully. At present, the field of culture change, including applied anthropology, is still young and immature. We have identified some regularities, however, and to that extent we can talk of limited predictions or probabilities as aids in making decisions.

For culture change to be successful, the problem of culture fit must be solved. Whether through incremental or systematic change, new cultures must be sufficiently integrated as wholes to enable them to function in an adequate manner. Further, to achieve this end, communication within a community and between one community and another must be effective. Effective communication can require the solution of a plethora of cultural problems ranging from difficulties with electronic media to the characteristics of status and role. If anthropologists cannot offer ready answers to all of the problems thus raised, at least we are prepared to gather the facts and examine them in the light of a growing body of accomplishments.

Finally, some anthropologists are as concerned as other scientists and humanists with that field of study identified as futuristics. Armageddon and the millennium are contrasting predictions we long have lived with. But an anthropological perspective makes one shy from such efforts to prophesy. The future is not preordained, and it therefore cannot be predicted with certainty. But while we cannot hope to prophesy, we can attempt to say something meaningful about how the future can be shaped, and that is a more satisfying kind of venture in many ways.

As I interpret the evidence, human ideas and individual genius rather than implacable economic or technological forces will determine our future. The difficulty is to assure that the people in power will have the genius and the ideas that truly will benefit mankind. That difficulty is not a problem for anthropologists alone. In fact, we deal with it primarily on the level of small communities and local governments. But insofar as we contribute, it constitutes a highly significant part of the anthropological endeavor.

An anthropological perspective will be different for every student of anthropology. But ultimately, we all see man in the same way. He is complex. He has potentialities for uniquely human achievements, but his capacity for cultural and personality developments always will have biological dimensions. And organically, the human body offers both possibilities for exciting achievements as well as limitations of sometimes depressing harshness. But above all, man alone has the capacity to study himself, to know himself. And to the extent that anthropology contributes importantly to knowing oneself, it offers a way to equip oneself to succeed in the most important career of all, which is living.

# Suggested Readings

## Chapter One: The Science of Man

*The Human Direction: An Evolutionary Approach to Social and Cultural Anthropology,* by James L. Peacock and A. Thomas Kirsch (paper, 1970). An introductory textbook.

*The Many Worlds of Man,* by Jack Conrad (paper, 1968). An introductory textbook.

*Cultural Ways: A Compact Introduction to Cultural Anthropology,* by Robert B. Taylor (paper, 1969). An introductory textbook.

*Invitation to Anthropology: A Guide to Basic Concepts,* by Douglas L. Oliver (paper, 1964). An introduction.

*Mirror for Man,* by Clyde Kluckhohn (paper, 1949). Still in print. A highly readable introduction with stress on the uses of anthropology.

*Horizons of Anthropology,* edited by Sol Tax (paper, 1964). A survey of current work, each chapter written by an expert.

*From Ape to Angel,* by H. R. Hays (paper, 1958). An introduction to the history of anthropology with emphasis upon individual anthropologists and human beings.

*In the Company of Man: Twenty Portraits of Anthropological Informants,* edited by Joseph B. Casagrande (paper, 1960). The anthropologist and his collaborators in the field.

*Return to Laughter: An Anthropological Novel,* by Elenore Smith Bowen (Laura Bohannon) (paper, 1954). The field experience as one anthropologist sees it.

*Stranger and Friend: The Way of an Anthropologist,* by Hortense Powdermaker (paper, 1966). The professional biography of an anthropologist.

## Chapter Two: The Garden of Eden

*Archaeology: An Illustrated Introduction,* by Liam de Paor (paper, 1967). A short introduction.

*Archaeology: An Introduction,* by Clement W. Meighan (paper, 1966). Well illustrated and well written.

*Prehistoric Men,* by Robert J. Braidwood (paper, 1967). A readable short introduction to archeology and its findings.

*Archaeology and Society,* by Grahame Clark (paper, 1957). Methods of archeological research.

*Mankind in the Making,* by William Howells (cloth, 1959). Introduction to human evolution.

*The Emergence of Man,* by John E. Pfeiffer (paper, 1969). An introduction to human evolution.

*Early Man,* by F. Clark Howell and the Editors of Time–Life Books (cloth, 1968). An introduction to human evolution.

*The Primates,* by Sarel Eimerl, Irven De Vore, and the Editors of Time–Life Books (cloth, 1965). A survey of Primate research.

*The Year of the Gorilla,* by George B. Schaller (paper, 1964). The rewards and the costs of field study by a zoologist.

## Chapter Three: The Real Adam

*Back of History,* by William Howells (paper, 1963). The origin of man to early civilization.

*The Old Stone Age,* by François Bordes (paper, 1968). Well illustrated.

*Palaeolithic Cave Art,* by Peter J. Ucko and André Rosenfeld (paper, 1967). Well illustrated.

*On the Track of Prehistoric Man,* by Herbert Kühn (paper, 1955). The thrill of discovery in an archeologist's lifetime of work on European cave art.

*The World of Ancient Man,* by I. W. Cornwall (paper, 1964). A reconstruction of prehistoric communities and their environments.

*The Stages of Human Evolution,* by C. Loring Brace (paper, 1967). A textbook account, though short.

*Prehistoric Societies,* by Grahame Clark and Stuart Piggott (cloth, 1967). Early man and his culture. Detailed but well written.

*The Lost Americans,* by Frank C. Hibben (paper, 1946). A pleasant-to-read book on Stone Age America.

*The Forest People: A Study of the Pygmies of the Congo,* by Colin M. Turnbull (paper, 1962). A hunting and gathering society.

*The Lost World of the Kalahari,* by Laurens Van der Post (paper, 1958). A traveler's account of the hunting and gathering Bushmen.

*The Australian Aborigines,* by A. P. Elkin (paper, 1964). A classic first published in 1938.

*The Tiwi of North Australia,* by C. W. M. Hart and Arnold R. Pilling (paper, 1959). An Australian hunting and gathering society as it is changing in our time.

## Chapter Four: The Mark of Cain

*Man Makes Himself,* by V. Gordon Childe (paper, 1951). The rise of civilization.

*What Happened in History,* by V. Gordon Childe (paper, 1954). The rise of civilization.

*The Human Factor in Changing Africa,* by Melville J. Herskovits (paper, 1962). Africa in anthropological perspective.

*The Nuer,* by E. S. Evans-Pritchard (paper, 1940). The classic study of a tribe of East Africa.

*The Barabaig: East African Cattle-Herders,* by George J. Klima (paper, 1969). A recent study.

*The Lugbara of Uganda,* by John Middleton (paper, 1965). An agricultural tribe of East Africa.

*Indians of the Americas,* by John Collier (paper, 1947). Early Indian culture and the effects of white contact.

*Man's Rise to Civilization as Shown by the Indians of North America from Primeval Times to the Coming of the Industrial State,* by Peter Farb (paper, 1968). Very readable.

*Yanomamö: The Fierce People,* by Napoleon A. Chagnon (paper, 1968). A very warlike tribe of South America.

*Sex and Temperament in Three Primitive Societies,* by Margaret Mead (paper, 1935). Tribal peoples of New Guinea.

*The High Valley,* by Kenneth E. Read (cloth, 1965). A New Guinea village people. Fascinating reading.

## Chapter Five: Noah's Curse

*Sons of the Shaking Earth,* by Eric Wolf (paper, 1959). A history of the people of Mexico and Guatemala.

*Tepoztlán: Village Life in Mexico,* by Oscar Lewis (paper, 1960). Peasant life in our time.

*Juan the Chamula: An Ethnological Re-Creation of the Life of a Mexican Indian,* by Ricardo Pozas (paper, 1962). A peasant.

*The Origins of Oriental Civilization,* by Walter A. Fairservis, Jr. (paper, 1959). An archeological reconstruction.

*Hill Farms and Padi Fields: Life in Mainland Southeast Asia,* by Robbins Burling (paper, 1965). A part of contemporary peasant Asia.

*The House of Lim: A Study of a Chinese Farm Family,* by Margery Wolf (paper, 1968). A peasant village on Taiwan today.

*The Dawn of European Civilization,* by V. Gordon Childe (paper, 1957). Peasant culture in archeological perspective.

*Inis Beag: Isle of Ireland,* by John C. Messenger (paper, 1969). A peasant village today.

*A Spanish Tapestry: Town and Country in Castile,* by Michael Kenny (paper, 1966). Village and city in contemporary Spain.

*Japan's Invisible Race: Caste in Culture and Personality,* edited by George De Vos and Hiroshi Wagatsuma (paper, 1968). The effect of discrimination on individual performance.

*The Concept of Race,* edited by Ashley Montagu (paper, 1964). An attack on old ideas about racial biology.


## Chapter Six: The Promised Land


*Traditional Cultures and the Impact of Technological Change,* by George M. Foster (cloth, 1962). What the anthropologist can say about culture change.

*Man Takes Charge,* by Charles Erasmus (paper, 1961). An assessment of applied anthropology.

*Blossoms in the Dust: The Human Factor in Indian Development,* by Kusum Nair (paper, 1961). A survey of culture change in India graphically told by an Indian journalist.

*Behind Mud Walls—1930–1960,* by William and Charlotte Wiser (paper, 1963). Culture change in a village in India.

*Report from a Chinese Village,* by Jan Myrdal (paper, 1965). A northern Chinese village transformed under communist leadership.

*K'un Shen: A Taiwan Village,* by Norma Diamond (paper, 1969). A village under Nationalist Chinese leadership.

*Changing Japan,* by Edward Norbeck (paper, 1965). Urban and rural contrasts in contemporary Japan.

*The Passing of Traditional Society: Modernizing the Middle East,* by Daniel Lerner (paper, 1958). Changing villages.

*From Tribe to Nation in Africa,* edited by Ronald Cohen and John Middleton (paper, 1970). The transformation of traditional communities into the parts of modern nations.

*Social Change,* by H. Ian Hogbin (cloth, 1958). Modernization in Oceania.

*Culture against Man,* by Jules Henry (paper, 1963). An anthropologist examines American culture.

## Chapter Seven: Armageddon

*The Marxists,* by C. Wright Mills (paper, 1962). Marx and his successors in the view of a sociologist.

*Evolution and Culture,* edited by Marshall D. Sahlins and Elman R. Service (cloth, 1960). A small but provocative book.

*The Science of Culture,* by Leslie White (paper, 1949). A classic work on cultural evolution.

*Man's Way: A Preface to the Understanding of Human Society,* by Walter Goldschmidt (paper, 1959). An effort to put the present in evolutionary perspective.

*Continuities in Cultural Evolution,* by Margaret Mead (paper, 1964). Evolutionary theory as a guide to the future.

# Footnotes

## Chapter One: The Science of Man

1. Robert H. Lowie, *The History of Ethnological Theory* (New York: Holt, Rinehart and Winston, 1937), p. 3.

2. Clyde Kluckhohn and William Kelly, "The Concept of Culture," *The Science of Man in the World Crisis*, ed. Ralph Linton (New York: Columbia University Press, 1945), p. 97.

3. Alfred Lewis Kroeber, *Anthropology* (New York: Harcourt Brace Jovanovich, 1948), p. 253.

4. Alfred Lewis Kroeber and Clyde Kluckhohn, *Culture: A Critical Review of Concepts and Definitions* (New York: Random House, 1963), p. 3.

5. Edward Burnett Tylor, *The Origins of Culture* (New York: Harper & Row, 1958), p. 1. (Originally published as Chapters 1–10 of *Primitive Culture* [London: John Murray, 1871].)

6. Arnold Van Gennep, *Les rites de passage* (Paris: É. Nourry, 1909). See also, The Rites of Passage (Chicago: University of Chicago Press, 1960).

7. Pertti J. Pelto, *Individualism in Skolt Lapp Society* (*Kansatieteellinen Arkisto* 16) (Helsinki: Suomen Muinaismuistoyhdistys [Finnish Antiquities Society], 1962), p. 109.

8. John W. M. Whiting, "The Cross-Cultural Method," *Handbook of Social Psychology*, ed. Gardner Lindzey (Cambridge, Mass.: Addison-Wesley Publishing Co., 1954); Gary Schwartz and Don Merten, "Social Identity and Expressive Symbols: The Meaning of an Initiation Ritual," *American Anthropologist*, Vol. 70, No. 6 (1968).

9. Bronislaw Malinowski, *Argonauts of the Western Pacific* (New York: E. P. Dutton & Co., 1961), p. xv. (First published in 1922.)

10. See Robert H. Lowie, *An Introduction to Cultural Anthropology*, rev. ed. (New York: Holt, Rinehart and Winston, 1940).

11. Malinowski, pp. 8–17, 81–84.

## Chapter Two: The Garden of Eden

1. Vincent M. Sarich, "The Origin of the Hominids: An Immunological Approach," *Perspectives on Human Evolution I*, ed. S. L. Washburn and Phyllis C. Jay (New York: Holt, Rinehart and Winston, 1968).

2. See John Buettner-Janusch, *Origins of Man: Physical Anthropology* (New York: John Wiley, 1966); William Howells, *Mankind in the Making: The Story of Human*

*Evolution* (New York: Doubleday & Co., 1959); Bernard Campbell, *Human Evolution: An Introduction to Man's Adaptations* (Chicago: Aldine Publishing Co., 1966).

3. See John E. Pfeiffer, *The Emergence of Man* (New York: Harper & Row, 1969); Ashley Montagu, *Man: His First Million Years,* rev. ed. (New York: New American Library, 1962); Marcellin Boule and Henri V. Vallois, *Fossil Men* (New York: Dryden Press, 1957).

4. See C. Loring Brace, *The Stages of Human Evolution: Human and Cultural Origins* (Englewood Cliffs, N.J.: Prentice-Hall, 1967).

5. Wilfred E. Le Gros Clark, *Man-Apes or Ape-Men? The Story of Discoveries in Africa* (New York: Holt, Rinehart and Winston, 1967).

6. Buettner-Janusch, p. 146.

7. Jane Goodall, "My Life among Wild Chimpanzees," *National Geographic,* Vol. 124, No. 2 (1963); Sarel Eimerl and Irven De Vore, *The Primates* (New York: Time-Life Books, 1965), pp. 67–70, 153–154.

8. Raymond A. Dart, "The Osteodontokeratic Culture of *Australopithecus prometheus,*" *Transvaal Museum Memoirs,* No. 10 (1957); "Bone Tools and Porcupine Gnawing," *American Anthropologist,* Vol. 60, No. 4 (1958); Le Gros Clark, pp. 112–124.

9. Elwyn L. Simons, "Some Fallacies in the Study of Hominid Phylogeny," in Washburn and Jay.

10. Simons, p. 38.


## Chapter Three: The Real Adam


1. William Howells, *Mankind in the Making: The Story of Evolution* (New York: Doubleday & Co., 1959), pp. 151–174; Wilfred E. Le Gros Clark, *The Fossil Evidence for Human Evolution,* 2nd. ed. (Chicago: University of Chicago Press, 1964); William Howells, "Homo Erectus," *Scientific American,* Vol. 215, No. 5 (1966).

2. Sherwood L. Washburn, "The New Physical Anthropology," *Transactions of the New York Academy of Sciences,* Series II, Vol. 13 (1951).

3. Sherwood L. Washburn, "An Ape's-Eye View of Human Evolution," *Evolutionary Anthropology: A Reader in Human Biology,* ed. Hermann K. Bleitreu (Boston: Allyn and Bacon, 1969); Sherwood L. Washburn and Irven De Vore, "Social Behavior of Baboons and Early Man," *Readings in Physical Anthropology,* ed. Thomas W. McKern (Englewood Cliffs, N.J.: Prentice-Hall, 1966).

4. See Earnest A. Hooton, *Up from the Ape* (New York: Macmillan Co., 1947), p. 304.

5. Sherwood L. Washburn, "An Ape's-Eye View of Human Evolution," Jane B. Lancaster, "Primate Communication Systems and the Emergence of Human Language," *Primates: Studies in Adaptation and Variability,* ed. Phyllis C. Jay (New York: Holt, Rinehart and Winston, 1968); Macdonald Critchley, "The Evolution of Man's Capactiy for Language," *The Evolution of Man,* ed. Sol Tax (Chicago: University of Chicago Press, 1960).

6. Clarence R. Carpenter, *Field Study in Siam of the Behavior and Social Relations of the Gibbon (Hylobates lar),* Comparative Psychology Monographs, Vol. 16, No. 5 (1940).

7. J. Bronowski and U. Bellugi, "Language, Name, and Concept," *Science,* Vol. 168 (1970).

8. "The Chimp Who Can Read," *San Francisco Chronicle,* July 22, 1970, pp. 1, 22.

9. Charles F. Hockett and Robert Ascher, "The Human Revolution," *Current Anthropology,* Vol. 5, No. 3 (1964).

10. Marvin Harris, *Culture, Man, and Nature: An Introduction to General Anthropology* (New York: Thomas Y. Crowell Co., 1971), pp. 119–120.

11. Noam Chomsky, *Syntactic Structures* (The Hague: Mouton, 1957); *Aspects of the Theory of Syntax* (Cambridge, Mass.: MIT Press, 1965).

12. Emmon Bach, "On Some Recurrent Types of Transformations," *Georgetown University Monograph Series on Languages and Linguistics*, Vol. 18, pp. 3–18.

13. Joseph H. Greenberg, "Some Universals of Grammar with Particular Reference to the Order of Meaningful Elements," *Universals of Language*, ed. Joseph H. Greenberg (Cambridge, Mass.: MIT Press, 1963), pp. 58–90; Mary Le Cron Foster, "Explorations in Semantic Phylogeny," paper read at the 69th annual meeting of the American Anthropological Association, San Diego, Calif., November 1970. See also Emmon Bach and Robert T. Harms, eds., *Universals in Linguistic Theory* (New York: Holt, Rinehart and Winston, 1968).

14. Edward Sapir, *Language* (New York: Harcourt Brace Jovanovich, 1921), p. 232.

15. John B. Carroll, ed., *Language, Thought, and Reality: Selected Writings of Benjamin Lee Whorf* (Cambridge, Mass.: MIT Press, 1956), pp. 135–136.

16. See Stephen A. Tyler, ed., *Cognitive Anthropology* (New York: Holt, Rinehart and Winston, 1969).

17. See Brent Berlin, "A Universalist-Evolutionary Approach in Ethnographic Semantics," and Paul Kay, "Some Theoretical Implications of Ethnographic Semantics," *Current Directions in Anthropology* (bulletin of the American Anthropological Association), Vol. 3, No. 3, Part 2 (1970), pp. 3–18, 19–34.

18. Howells, *Mankind in the Making*, pp. 189–204; Hooton, pp. 319–339; F. Clark Howell, "The Evolutionary Significance of Variation and Varieties of 'Neanderthal' Man," *The Quarterly Review of Biology*, Vol. 32, No. 4 (1957).

19. R. S. Solecki, "Three Neanderthal Skeletons from Shanidar Cave, Northern Iraq," *Smithsonian Report*, Publication No. 4414, 1959–1960; Carleton S. Coon, *The Origin of Races* (New York: Alfred A. Knopf, 1963), pp. 561–565.

20. C. Loring Brace, "The Fate of the 'Classic' Neanderthals: A Consideration of Hominid Catastrophism," *Current Anthropology*, Vol. 5, No. 1 (1964).

21. Jacquetta Hawkes and Leonard Woolley, *History of Mankind*, Vol. 1, *Prehistory and the Beginnings of Civilization* (New York: Harper & Row, 1963), pp. 63–103; François Bordes, *The Old Stone Age* (New York: McGraw-Hill Book Co., 1968).

22. Peter J. Ucko and Andrée Rosenfeld, *Paleolithic Cave Art* (New York: McGraw-Hill Book Co., 1967); Herbert Kühn, *On the Track of Prehistoric Man* (New York: Random House, 1955).

23. Grahame Clark and Stuart Piggot, *Prehistoric Societies* (New York: Alfred A. Knopf, 1967), pp. 64–97.

24. Kühn, pp. 95–97.

25. Grahame Clark, *World Prehistory—An Outline* (Cambridge: Cambridge University Press, 1961), pp. 63–75; Robert J. Braidwood, *Prehistoric Men*, 7th ed. (Chicago: Scott, Foresman and Co., 1967), pp. 81–93.

26. Cited in Sherwood L. Washburn and C. S. Lancaster, "The Evolution of Hunting," *Man the Hunter*, ed. Richard Lee and Irven De Vore (Chicago: Aldine Publishing Co., 1968), p. 295.

27. Washburn and Lancaster, p. 216.

## Chapter Four: The Mark of Cain

1. Leonard Berkowitz, cited in Ralph L. Holloway, Jr., "Human Aggression: The Need for a Species-Specific Framework," *War: The Anthropology of Armed Conflict*

*and Aggression,* ed. Morton Fried, Marvin Harris, and Robert Murphy (Garden City, N.Y.: Natural History Press, 1968), p. 32.

2. See Elman R. Service, *Primitive Social Organization: An Evolutionary Perspective* (New York: Random House, 1962); Elman R. Service, *The Hunters* (Englewood Cliffs, N.J.: Prentice-Hall, 1966).

3. Service, *The Hunters,* p. 55.

4. Jacquetta Hawkes and Leonard Woolley, *History of Mankind,* Vol. 1, *Prehistory and the Beginnings of Civilization* (New York: Harper & Row, 1963), pp. 219–352; V. Gordon Childe, *Man Makes Himself* (New York: New American Library, 1951), pp. 59–113.

5. Marshall D. Sahlins, *Tribesmen* (Englewood Cliffs, N.J.: Prentice-Hall, 1968).

6. William Howells, *Back of History,* rev. ed. (New York: Doubleday & Co., 1963); Grahame Clark, *World Prehistory—An Outline* (Cambridge: Cambridge University Press, 1961); Ralph Linton, *The Tree of Culture* (New York: Alfred A. Knopf, 1955).

7. Robert Ardrey, *African Genesis: A Personal Investigation into the Animal Origins and Nature of Man* (New York: Dell Publishing Co., 1961); Robert Ardrey, *The Territorial Imperative: A Personal Inquiry into the Animal Origins of Property and Nations* (New York: Dell Publishing Co., 1966); Desmond Morris, *The Naked Ape* (New York: Dell Publishing Co., 1967); Konrad Z. Lorenz, *On Aggression* (New York: Harcourt Brace Jovanovich, 1966). For a contrary view, see Santiago Genovés, *Is Peace Inevitable? Aggression, Evolution, and Human Destiny* (New York: Walker & Co., 1970).

8. George V. Shkurkin, personal communication.

9. Sarel Eimerl and Irven De Vore, *The Primates* (New York: Time-Life Books, 1965), pp. 105–114.

10. E. E. Evans-Pritchard, *The Nuer: A Description of the Modes of Livelihood and Political Institutions of a Nilotic People* (Oxford: Clarendon Press, 1940), pp. 150–152.

11. Napoleon Chagnon, *Yanomamö: The Fierce People* (New York: Holt, Rinehart and Winston, 1968), pp. 119–137.

12. Sahlins, pp. 4–13.

13. See Evans-Pritchard, *The Nuer.*

14. See Robert H. Lowie, *Indians of the Plains* (New York: McGraw-Hill Book Co., 1954); Clark Wissler, *North American Indians of the Plains* (New York: American Museum of Natural History, 1927); Alvin M. Josephy, Jr., *The Indian Heritage of America* (New York: Alfred A. Knopf, 1970), pp. 110–123; Ruth M. Underhill, *Red Man's America: A History of Indians in the United States* (Chicago: University of Chicago Press, 1953), pp. 144–185.

15. Kaj Birket-Smith, *Primitive Man and His Ways: Patterns of Life in Some Native Societies* (New York: New American Library, 1963), p. 67.

16. Alfred L. Kroeber, "Zuñi Kin and Clan," *Anthropological Papers of the American Museum of Natural History,* Vol. 18, 1917.

17. Evans-Pritchard, pp. 249–266.

18. Lowie, p. 101, adapted.


## Chapter Five: Noah's Curse


1. See V. Gordon Childe, *What Happened in History* (Baltimore, Md.: Penguin Books, 1942).

2. Marshall D. Sahlins, *Tribesmen* (Englewood Cliffs, N.J.: Prentice-Hall, 1968), p. 5.

3. Pitirim A. Sorokin, *Social and Cultural Dynamics*, Vol. 3 (Totowa, New Jersey: Bedminster, 1937–1941), p. 352.

4. A. L. Kroeber, *Anthropology* (New York: Harcourt Brace Jovanovich, 1948), pp. 728–729.

5. Arthur R. Jensen, "How Much Can We Boost IQ and Scholastic Achievement?" *Harvard Educational Review*, Vol. 39 (1969).

6. Ruth Benedict, *Race: Science and Politics*, rev. ed. (New York: Viking Press, 1943), p. 72. See also Aline H. Kidd, "The Culture-Fair Aspects of Cattell's Test of J: Culture-Free," *Journal of Genetic Psychology*, Vol. 101 (1962), pp. 343–345.

7. Cited in William F. Brazziel, "Perspective on the Jensen Affair," *Childhood Education*, Vol. 46, No. 7 (1970), pp. 371–373. See also Gilbert Voyat, "IQ: God-Given or Man-Made?" *Saturday Review*, May 17, 1869, pp. 73–75, 86–87.

8. Benedict, p. 76.

9. Thomas Bendyshe, ed., *The Anthropological Treatises of J. F. Blumenbach* (London: Longmans, Green & Co., 1865).

10. Kroeber, pp. 124–176.

11. Carleton S. Coon, *The Origin of Races* (New York: Alfred A. Knopf, 1963).

12. Earnest A. Hooton, *Up from the Ape* (New York: Macmillan Co., 1947), p. 612.

13. Hooton, p. 633.

14. Hooton, p. 619.

15. Frank B. Livingstone, "On the Nonexistence of Human Races," *The Concept of Race*, ed. Ashley Montagu (New York: Collier Books, 1969).

16. Ashley Montagu, "The Concept of Race in the Human Species in the Light of Genetics," p. 6, *The Concept of Race*.

17. C. Loring Brace, "A Nonracial Approach towards the Understanding of Human Diversity," p. 107, *The Concept of Race*.

18. Brace, pp. 108–119.

19. Brace, pp. 124–139.

20. Brace, p. 134.

21. John Buettner-Janusch, *Origins of Man: Physical Anthropology* (New York: John Wiley, 1966), pp. 539–545; Sherwood L. Washburn, "The Study of Race," *The Concept of Race*, p. 248.

22. Robert D. McCracken, "Adult Lactose Tolerance," *Journal of the American Medical Association*, Vol. 213, No. 13 (1970).

23. Theodosius Dobzhansky and M. F. Ashley Montagu, "Natural Selection and the Mental Capacities of Mankind," *Science*, Vol. 105, No. 2736 (1947), p. 588.

24. Dobzhansky and Montagu, p. 589.

25. George DeVos and Hiroshi Wagatsuma, *Japan's Invisible Race: Caste in Culture and Personality* (Berkeley: University of California Press, 1967).

26. DeVos and Wagatsuma, p. 231.

27. DeVos and Wagatsuma, p. 237.

## Chapter Six: The Promised Land

1. Clifford Geertz, "Studies in Peasant Life: Community and Society," *Biennial Review of Anthropology—1961*, Bernard J. Siegel, ed. (Stanford, Calif.: Stanford University Press, 1962), p. 1.

2. George M. Foster, "Introduction: What Is a Peasant?" *Peasant Society: A Reader*, Jack M. Potter, May N. Diaz, and George M. Foster, eds. (Boston: Little, Brown & Co., 1967), p. 6.

3. Robert Redfield, *Peasant Society and Culture: An Anthropological Approach to Civilization* (Chicago: University of Chicago Press, 1956), p. 112.

4. Eric R. Wolf, *Peasants* (Englewood Cliffs, N.J.: Prentice-Hall, 1966), pp. 12–13.

5. Oscar Lewis, *La Vida: A Puerto Rican Family in the Culture of Poverty—San Juan and New York* (New York: Random House, 1965), pp. XLII–LII.

6. Lewis, p. XLVII.

7. George M. Foster, *Applied Anthropology* (Boston: Little, Brown & Co., 1969). See also George M. Foster, *Traditional Cultures and the Impact of Technological Change* (New York: Harper & Row, 1962).

8. Foster, *Applied Anthropology*, pp. 8–9.

9. Robert T. Anderson, "Eskimo Reindeer Herding: A Problem in Applied Anthropology," *Anthropological Quarterly*, Vol. 32, No. 2 (1959).

10. Foster, *Traditional Cultures*, pp. 162–176.

11. Foster, *Traditional Cultures*, pp. 120–142.

12. William McCord, *The Springtime of Freedom: The Evolution of Developing Societies* (New York: Oxford University Press, 1965), p. 10.

13. Chester L. Hunt, "Cultural Barriers to Point Four," *Underdeveloped Areas: A Book of Readings*, ed. Lyle W. Shannon (New York: Harper & Row, 1957), p. 318.

14. Cited in William Hinton, *Fanshen: A Documentary of Revolution in a Chinese Village* (New York: Random House, 1968), p. 107.

15. Irving Louis Horowitz, *Three Worlds of Development: The Theory and Practice of International Stratification* (New York: Oxford University Press, 1966), p. 18.

16. See M. N. Srinivas, *Social Change in Modern India* (Berkeley: University of California Press, 1969), pp. 75–84; Beatrice Pitney Lamb, *India: A World in Transition*, rev. ed. (New York: Praeger Publishers, 1966), p. 258.

17. Melville J. Herskovits, *Man and His Works: The Science of Cultural Anthropology* (New York: Alfred A. Knopf, 1950), p. 580.

18. Lamb, pp. 258–261; John P. Lewis, *Quiet Crisis in India: Economic Development and American Policy* (Garden City, N.Y.: Doubleday & Co., 1964), pp. 168–177; Ronald Segal, *The Anguish of India* (New York: New American Library, 1965), pp. 195–197; Hugh Tinker, *India and Pakistan: A Political Analysis* (New York: Praeger Publishers, 1962), pp. 191–196, 198–201.

19. Oscar Lewis, *Village Life in Northern India* (New York: Random House, 1965), p. 151.

20. Albert Mayer et al., *Pilot Project, India: The Story of Rural Development at Etawah, Uttar Pradesh* (Berkeley: University of California Press, 1958). See also William H. Wiser and Charlotte Viall Wiser, *Behind Mud Walls, 1930–1960* (Berkeley: University of California Press, 1963).

21. Robert T. Anderson, *Denmark: The Success of a Developing Nation* (Cambridge, Mass.: Schenkman Publishing Co., to appear); Robert T. Anderson, "The Vanishing Villages of Denmark," *Anthropologica*, N.S., Vol. 12, No. 1 (1970).

22. Margaret Mead, *New Lives for Old: Cultural Transformation—Manus, 1928–1953* (New York: Dell Publishing Co., 1966). See also Margaret Mead, *Growing Up in New Guinea: A Comparative Study of Primitive Education* (New York: William Morrow & Co., 1962). (First published in 1930.)

23. Mead, *Growing Up in New Guinea*, p. 42.

24. Mead, *New Lives for Old*, p. 173.

25. Mead, *New Lives for Old*, pp. 411–422.

26. For example, H. Ian Hogbin, *Social Change* (London: C. H. Watts & Co., 1958), p. 13.

27. See Mead, *New Lives for Old*, pp. 411, 415.

28. Robert T. Anderson and Barbara G. Anderson, *The Vanishing Village: A Danish Maritime Community* (Seattle: University of Washington Press, 1964).

29. See Kung-chuan Hsiao, *Rural China: Imperial Control in the Nineteenth Century* (Seattle: University of Washington Press, 1960).

30. John King Fairbank, *The United States and China,* rev. ed. (New York: Viking Press, 1962), pp. 149–228.

31. See Hinton, *Fanshen;* Jan Myrdal, *Report from a Chinese Village* (New York: New American Library, 1966); Isabel and David Crook, *Revolution in a Chinese Village: Ten Mile Inn* (London: Routledge & Kegan Paul, 1959); William Robert Geddes, *Peasant Life in Communist China,* Society for Applied Anthropology, Monograph No. 6 (1963); C. K. Yang, *A Chinese Village in Early Communist Transition* (Boston: Technology Press, 1959).

## Chapter Seven: Armageddon

1. Cited in Reinhard Bendix, *Max Weber: An Intellectual Portrait* (Garden City, N.Y.: Doubleday & Co., 1960), p. 9.

2. C. Wright Mills, *The Marxists* (New York: Dell Publishing Co., 1962), p. 13.

3. Karl R. Popper, *The Open Society and Its Enemies* (London: Rutledge and Kegan Paul, 1950), p. 275.

4. Mills, pp. 24–27.

5. Lynn White, Jr., "The Historical Roots of Our Ecologic Crisis," paper read at the 133rd meeting of the American Association for the Advancement of Science, December 26, 1966.

6. Popper, pp. 277–281.

7. Cited in Popper, 331.

8. Marshall D. Sahlins and Elman R. Service, eds., *Evolution and Culture* (Ann Arbor: University of Michigan Press, 1960), pp. 12–44.

9. Julian H. Steward, *Theory of Culture Change: The Methodology of Multilinear Evolution* (Urbana: University of Illinois Press, 1955), pp. 11–29 et passim.

10. Steward, pp. 122–142.

11. Leslie A. White, *The Science of Culture: A Study of Man and Civilization* (New York: Grove Press, 1949), p. 367.

12. White, pp. 363–393; Leslie A. White, *The Evolution of Culture: The Development of Civilization to the Fall of Rome* (New York: McGraw-Hill Book Co., 1959), pp. 38–39, 42.

13. Sahlins and Service, pp. 22–23.

14. Sahlins and Service, p. 31.

15. Sahlins and Service, p. 31.

16. A. L. Kroeber, foreword to Rushton Coulborn, ed., *Feudalism in History* (Hamden, Conn.: Archon Books, 1965), p. VIII.

17. Coulborn, passim.

18. Robert H. Lowie, *Social Oraganization* (New York: Holt, Rinehart and Winston, 1948), p. 24.

19. White, *The Science of Culture,* p. 366.

20. White, *The Science of Culture,* p. 366.

21. See Mills, pp. 132–158.

22. Cited in Sahlins and Service, p. 100.

23. Cited in Sahlins nd Service, p. 109.

24. Sahlins and Service, pp. 93–122.

25. Cited in Sahlins and Service, p. 96.

26. Sahlins and Service, p. 97.

27. Margaret Mead, *Continuities in Cultural Evolution* (New Haven, Conn.: Yale University Press, 1964).

28. Mead, pp. 265–266.

29. James A. Michener, *Iberia: Spanish Travels and Reflections* (Greenwich, Conn.: Fawcett Publications, 1968), p. 829.

30. Collin Rosser, cited in William McCord, *The Springtime of Freedom: The Evolution of Developing Societies* (New York: Oxford University Press, 1965), pp. 26–27.

31. Kusum Nair, *Blossoms in the Dust: The Human Factor in Indian Development* (New York: Praeger Publishers, 1962), p. 125.

# Index

Intelligence tests, 68–69
Ishi, 6

Jensen, Arthur, 68

Kinship:
  in bands, 51
  clans, 57
  lineage, 57
  of man with other primates, 18
    (*see also* Hominid)
  system, 52
Kluckhohn, Clyde, 6
Knapper, 33
Kroeber, Alfred Lewis, 6, 60, 69, 70

Language, first appearance, 36
Lee, Richard B., 46
Lerner, Abba, 107
Lewis, Oscar, 81
Lineage, defined, 57
Linguistic universals, 38
Linnaeus, 17
Livingstone, Frank B., 72
Lorenz, Konrad, 55
Lowie, Robert H., 5, 103

Malinowski, Bronislaw, 10, 12, 93
Maoist era, 94
Mao Tse-tung, 87, 94, 105, 106
Marriage customs of patrilocality and
  exogamy, 51
Marx, Karl:
  and Engels, 103
  erred in predicting revolution in work-
    ing class, 105
  evolutionary theory of, 102
  social theory of, 98–100
Marxism:
  determinism in, 99
  evaluated in terms of evolutionary
    theory, 100
  as social theory, 99
McCord, William, 85
McCracken, Robert D., 74
Mead, Margaret:
  studies of Manus, 92–94
  theory of cultural evolution through
    genius, 108–109
Mesolithic period, 46–53
Mesozoic period, 15
Michener, James A., 109
Militarism, cost of, to a society, 67
  (*see also* Warfare)
Mills, C. Wright, 97, 99
Mindel, the, 25
Miocene Period, 20, 24
  dryopithecine in, 24
Modernization as distinct from westerni-
  zation, 86
Montagu, Ashley, 72, 75
Morgan, Lewis Henry, 4, 10
Morris, Desmond, 55
Music, first used as ritual, 45
Myrdal, Jan, 96

Nair, Kusum, 111
Natural selection, 72–73, 113
Neanderthal man, *see* Primates
Negroes in U.S., intelligence of, 68–69
Neolithic period, 53–62
Nuer of Africa:
  initiation rites, 9, 60
  patterns of warfare among, 55–58

Oligocene period, 20
  pithecine in, 22
  site in Fayum Depression of Egypt, 23

Paleoanthropology, 2–3
Paleocene period, 20, 21
Paleolithic period, 31–46
Paleozoic period, 16
Pastoralists appeared in Neolithic, 54
Peasants:
  in China, 94–96
  culture of, 66–68
  defined, 81
Pelto, Pertti J., 9
Plains Indians:
  initiation rites, 9
  social organization of, 58–60
  tribal associations of, 61–62
  warfare among, 58–60
Pleistocene period, 20, 25–29
  australopithecine in, 26
*Plesiadapsis,* 21
Pliocene period, 20, 24–25
  dryopithecine in, 24
  *Ramapithecus* in, 24
Pluvial periods, 26
Poor, urban, 80
Poverty, culture of, 81
Pre-Cambrian period, 16
Premack, David, 37
Primate grades:
  australopithecine, 26
  dryopithecine, 24, 27
  erectus, 32
  and levels of sociocultural integration,
    101
  neanderthalensis, 39–42
  pithecine, 22
  plesiadapidae, 21
  prosimian, 21
  ramapithecine (first hominid), 25, 26
  sapiens, 42
Primates, Eocene (prosimians):
  lemurs and tarsiers, 21
  *Smilodectes,* 21
  surviving to present, 22
Primates, Miocene:
  dryopithecine, 24, 27
  first tool use, 27
Primates, Oligocene (grade Pithecine):
  *Aegyptopithecus,* 23
  *Aeolopithecus,* 23
  *Amphipithecus,* 23
  *Apidium,* 23
  *Oligopithecus,* 23
  *Oreopithecus,* 23